THE TREASURE
OF MY CATHOLIC FAITH

NATIONAL CONSULTANTS FOR EDUCATION, INC.

CIRCLE
PRESS
SCHOLASTIC

Copyright © 2003 by National Consultants for Education, Inc. ALL RIGHTS RESERVED.

No part of this publication may be reproduced or stored in a retrieval system or transmitted in any form or by any means, electronic, mechanical, photocopying, recording or otherwise without prior written permission from National Consultants for Education, Inc. and Circle Media, Inc.

BOOK DESIGN   PPA Media

ILLUSTRATIONS   Dolores Cortes, Edmundo Santamaria.

ISBN 0-9743661-6-1

"The Ad Hoc Committee to Oversee the Use of the Catechism, United States Conference of Catholic Bishops, has found this catechetical text, copyright 2003, to be in conformity with the *Catechism of the Catholic Church*."

Anima Christi taken from "Catholic Household Blessings & Prayers"
© 1989 United States Conference of Catholic Bishops

Act of Faith, Hope and Love & *Eucharistic Hour Prayer* taken from
"The Handbook of Indulgences Norms & Grants"
© 1991 Catholic Book Publishing Co.

Psalm 8 taken from "The New American Bible"
© 1987 Catholic Book Publishing Co.

Printed in the United States of America

Published by Circle Press Scholastic, an imprint of Circle Press, a division of Circle Media, Inc.
For more information or to purchase this title contact:
Circle Press
PO Box 5425
Hamden, CT 06518-0425
www.catholictextbooks.org
888-881-0729

Disclaimer: The editor of this book has attempted to give proper credit to all sources used in the text and illustrations. Any miscredit or lack of credit is unintended and will be corrected in the next edition.

CONTENTS

CHAPTER 1

The Birth of Christ

CHAPTER 2

Christ's Infancy

CHAPTER 3

The Parables of the Kingdom

CHAPTER 4

Jesus, the Performer of Miracles

CHAPTER 5

Jesus' Friends

CHAPTER 6

The Last Supper

CHAPTER 7

The Passion

CHAPTER 8

The Resurrection

THE BIRTH OF CHRIST

Chapter 1

How did Mary Answer?

The Annunciation
Chapter 1, Lesson 1

Remember
**because he sinned, man couldn't go to heaven,
and so God promised to send a Savior.**
Now you're going to find out
how Mary helped God save mankind.

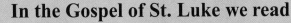

In the Gospel of St. Luke we read

"In the sixth month, the angel Gabriel was sent from God to a town of Galilee called Nazareth, to a virgin betrothed to a man named Joseph, of the house of David, and the virgin's name was Mary. And coming to her, he said, '*Hail, favored one! The Lord is with you.*' But she was greatly troubled at what was said and pondered what sort of greeting this might be.

"Then the angel said to her, '*Do not be afraid, Mary, for you have found favor with God. Behold, you will conceive in your womb and bear a son, and you shall name him Jesus. He will be great and will be called Son of the Most High, and the Lord God will give him the throne of David his father, and he will rule over the house of Jacob forever, and of his kingdom there will be no end.*' But Mary said to the angel, '*How can this be, since I have no relations with a man?*' And the angel said to her in reply, '*The Holy Spirit will come upon you, and the power of the Most High will overshadow you. Therefore the child to be born will be called holy, the Son of God. And behold, Elizabeth, your relative, has also conceived a son in her old age, and this is the sixth month for her who was called barren; for nothing will be impossible for God.*' Mary said, '**Behold, I am the handmaid of the Lord. May it be done to me according to your word.**' Then the angel departed from her."

Lk 1:26-38

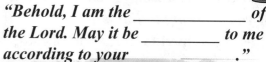

What we've read in the Gospel

Fill in the blanks.

"Do not be afraid, _____, for you have found favor with _____. Behold, you will conceive in your womb and bear a _____, and you shall name him _____."

"Behold, I am the _____ of the Lord. May it be _____ to me according to your _____."

The Archangel Gabriel

Mary

Answer the following questions.

What did the angel say to Mary?_____

_____

How did she react?_____

_____

What did she say to the angel in response?_____

_____

What does her response mean for us? _____

_____

Mary's Response

We can learn many things from Mary's response to the angel's words. Here are a few of the things we can learn.

OPENNESS: Mary was open to God's will for her, and ready to embrace it full of trust in him; and aware that nothing is impossible for him.

HUMILITY: Mary didn't think she was worthy of being chosen by God. She didn't understand why the angel would praise her as he did.

READINESS: Mary's response is immediate. She doesn't wait to think over what God is asking of her.

PURITY: Mary is full of grace, full of God, and born without the stain of original sin.

Find the dispositions that we can learn from Mary in this alphabet soup:

Openness • Humilty • Readiness • Purity

o	h	p	h	b	h	r
p	u	r	i	t	y	e
e	m	c	u	i	o	a
n	i	m	u	i	j	d
n	l	d	u	h	g	i
e	i	i	h	g	f	n
s	t	t	c	z	x	e
s	y	u	d	x	c	s
k	l	d	e	q	a	s

God sent us a Savior so we could all go to heaven and be happy with him forever. He knew that we needed such a Savior.

He sent him to us because Mary was ready and willing to help him save the world.

God wants to save you because he loves you very much. That's why he decided to become a man. The Incarnation is the mystery of the wonderful union of the human and divine natures in the one person of the Word. The Word, the second person of the Holy Trinity, became flesh by being born of the Virgin Mary.

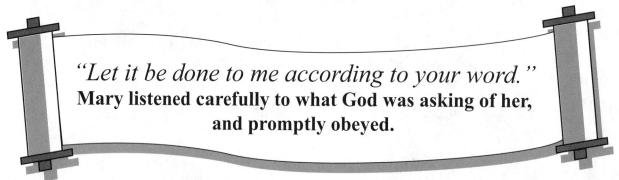

"Let it be done to me according to your word."
Mary listened carefully to what God was asking of her, and promptly obeyed.

By accepting and carrying out God's will, Mary showed that she loved God above all things.

Respond: In what situations is it hardest for someone your age to do God's will?	What do you think Mary would do in such situations?

Just like Mary, you can show God how much you love him by doing his will, by carrying out all that he is asking of you.

How can you know what he is asking of you? He lets you know through the Commandments, your parents, your teachers, and your priests, as well as the rules of your school.

What do they tell you?

your parents

_____
_____
_____
_____
_____

They tell you what God is asking of you.

your priests

_____
_____
_____
_____
_____

the Commandments

_____
_____
_____
_____

the rules of your school

_____
_____
_____
_____

your teachers

_____
_____
_____
_____

Every time you visit Jesus in the Eucharist, ask him to help you understand what God is asking of you.

Read the following sentences. Indicate whether each sentence talks about a child saying "yes" or "no" to God by connecting the sentence to the correct word.

Talks back to his parents.
Prays every day.
Shares his things.
Is very rude.
Doesn't do his homework.
Is very kind to others.
Tries to be helpful towards everyone.

Draw a picture of children in class doing God's will.

I'm going to show God how much I love him. I'm going to do his will just as Mary did.

Why do you do the things you do?
Underline the correct answers.

I should do my homework the best I can
- just to get good grades.
- to prepare myself and to be a better child of God.

I should obey my parents
- out of love for them and to please God.
- so I won't get punished.

I should go to Mass
- because all my friends go.
- out of love for Jesus in the Eucharist.

I should share with my friends
- so they'll share with me.
- so that I'll be like Jesus.

There's a prayer Mary likes very much because it reminds her of a very happy moment in her life, when the angel told her she was going to be the Mother of Jesus.

This prayer is called the "*Angelus*." Pray it together with your classmates.

The Angel spoke God's message to Mary.

And she conceived of the Holy Spirit.

Hail, Mary, full of grace...

"I am the lowly servant of the Lord."

Let it be done to me according to your word.

Hail, Mary, full of grace...

And the Word became flesh.

And lived among us.

The Pope prays the Angelus every day. On Sundays from his window overlooking St. Peter's Square, he prays it together with pilgrims from all over the world.

Hail, Mary, full of grace...

Pray for us, Holy Mother of God.
That we may become worthy of the promises of Christ.

Let us pray: *Lord, fill our hearts with your grace: once, through the message of an angel you revealed to us the incarnation of your Son; now, through his suffering and death lead us to the glory of his resurrection. We ask this through Christ our Lord.* Amen.

Glory to the Father, and to the Son, and to the Holy Spirit.
As it was in the beginning, is now, and will be forever. Amen.
(three times)

Don't forget

- The angel brought **Mary** a message of **salvation.**
- Mary **loved God above all things,** and showed her love by fulfilling his will with **humility, readiness, purity, and openness.**
- Mary **trusted** in God and readily offered herself to help him save mankind.
- God wants to save us because he **loves** us.
- Jesus became a man in order to **save** us.

Knowing my faith

Whom did God choose to collaborate with him in bringing about the mystery of the Incarnation?
He chose the Blessed Virgin Mary.

Living my faith

God is asking me to work together with him and help him.
Following Mary's example, I'm going to obey God

- **at home:** I'm going to be obedient towards my parents because I love them and they only want what is best for me because God lets me know his will for me through them, even if sometimes I don't like what they ask me to do.
- **at school:** I'm going to put extra effort into my homework, showing God that I love him.
- **as a Catholic Christian:** I'm going to go to the chapel to ask God to help me carry out his will for me.

What a long trip!

The Visitation
Chapter 1, Lesson 2

Remember
the angel told Mary that Elizabeth was going to have a son Mary decided to go and help her.

Now you're going to discover
helping and serving others is one way to live out our faith.

In the Gospel we read

"During those days Mary set out and traveled to the hill country in haste to a town of Judah, where she entered the house of Zechariah and greeted Elizabeth. When Elizabeth heard Mary's greeting, the infant leaped in her womb, and Elizabeth, filled with the Holy Spirit, cried out in a loud voice and said, '*Most blessed are you among women, and blessed is the fruit of your womb. And how does this happen to me, that the mother of my Lord should come to me? For at the moment the sound of your greeting reached my ears, the infant in my womb leaped for joy. Blessed are you who believed that what was spoken to you by the Lord would be fulfilled.*' And Mary said, '*My soul proclaims the greatness of the Lord; my spirit rejoices in God my savior. For he has looked upon his handmaid's lowliness; behold, from now on will all ages call me blessed. The Mighty One has done great things for me, and holy is his name. his mercy is from age to age to those who fear him. He has shown might with his arm, dispersed the arrogant of mind and heart. He has thrown down the rulers from their thrones but lifted up the lowly. The hungry he has filled with good things; the rich he has sent away empty. He has helped Israel his servant, remembering his mercy, according to his promise to our fathers, to Abraham and to his descendants forever.*' Mary remained with her about three months and then returned to her home."

Lk 1:39-56

- **Mary thought of others before herself.**
- **She did not think of the discomfort of the journey; she went to help Elizabeth.**
- **Mary's great faith leads her to give her life to God in what he asks of her.**
- **Mary's response was to love and serve others.**
- **Elizabeth receives Mary and the Savior with great joy.**

What do you think Mary did once she got to Elizabeth's house?

What she most surely did	What she certainly did not do
1. **Cheerfully** helped her cousin.	1. **Complain** about the difficulties.
2. _____	2. _____
3. _____	3. _____

What do think the following statements mean? Underline the correct answers.

"My soul proclaims the greatness of the Lord"
- Mary didn't understand what the angel told her.
- Mary was singing God's praises.

"For he has looked upon his handmaid's lowliness"
- Mary recognized her smallness next to God's greatness.
- Mary had no money.

"The Mighty One has done great things for me"
- God made Mary very pretty.
- Mary would give birth to the Savior.

"He has ... lifted up the lowly"
- Jesus would be born among kings.
- Christ would be born among common people.

"...according to his promise to our fathers"
- God promised to punish Adam.
- God promised to send a Savior to Abraham.

"Blessed are you who believe."

With these words Elizabeth rejoiced over Mary's faith in God, and Mary responded with a song of praise to God. We call her song the *Magnificat.*

Fill in the missing words of the Magnificat, and then recite it together with your classmates.

'My soul proclaims the greatness of the _____; my spirit rejoices in God my _____. For he has looked upon his handmaid's _____; behold, from now on will all ages call me _____. The Mighty One has done _____ things for me, and holy is his name.'

His mercy is from age to age to those who fear him. He has shown _____ with his arm, dispersed the arrogant of mind and heart.

He has thrown down the _____ from their thrones but lifted up the lowly. The _____ he has filled with good things; the rich he has sent away empty.

He has helped Israel his servant, remembering his mercy, according to his _____ to our fathers, to Abraham and to his descendants forever

great

blessed

hungry

Lord

might

savior

rulers

lowliness

promise

Write your own song praising God.

Do you remember Christ's New Commandment, the Commandment of love?
Complete this sentence.

"Love one another _____ *"*

A life dedicated to serving others

Blessed Teresa of Calcutta was born on August 26,
1910 in Albania. She was born as Ines Bojaxhiu. When
she was eighteen years old, Ines decided to give her
life to God and went to Ireland to join the Sisters of
Loretto. Later she was transferred to Calcutta, India,
where she spent 20 years teaching as a nun.
One day, as she went to a retreat, she was overcome
with compassion for all the abandoned and dying
people in the streets of Calcutta. She felt God calling
her to console and comfort them.
With the Pope's approval, she founded the
"Missionaries of Charity" sisters, dedicated to serving
the poorest of the poor. Together with her sisters,
Mother Teresa founded relief centers and shelters all
over the world. In 1979 she received the Nobel Peace
Prize. But that is nothing compared to the reward God
had waiting for her in heaven, because of her great
faith and love. She died on September 5, 1997 and was
proclaimed Blessed on October 19, 2003.

*"Our faith is nothing other than a
gospel of love, showing man how
much God loves him, and showing
man that God expects to be loved
in return."*

Blessed Teresa of Calcutta

Answer the questions and discuss them with your classmates:

1. Do you think Blessed Teresa was like Mary in any way? _____

2. To what did Blessed Teresa dedicate her life? _____

3. Why? _____

4. What are some of the things that must be hard about her work?_____

5. What enabled her to keep going despite such difficulties?_____

6. What do you think she did to be so close to God? _____

7. How did she show God her love for him?_____

Use your imagination.

What do you think Mary was like when she was your age?	Write down here how you can be just like she was.

Mary's trip to Elizabeth's house was not an easy one. The road was not a smooth highway, and she didn't have a luxury car. She traveled dirt roads through the mountains riding on a donkey.

You too are going to come across difficulties as you go through life striving to love God and serve others. Write down what you think will be some of your biggest difficulties, and what you can do to overcome them.

Difficulties:	How I will face them.

Ask God to help you be strong.

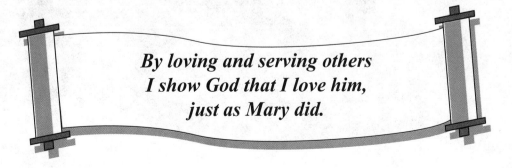

By loving and serving others
I show God that I love him,
just as Mary did.

Don't forget

- To have faith means to **believe** in God and to **live** as he taught us.
- **Faith** is essential for Christians and *necessary* for our salvation.
- Mary **lived by faith** and offered her entire life to God.
- Mary showed how much she **believed** in and **loved** God by **loving and serving** others, as she did her cousin Elizabeth.

Knowing my faith

Is Mary really and truly the "Mother of God?"
Yes, because her Son, Jesus, is God himself.

How did Mary collaborate in the salvation of mankind?
She did this through her faith and voluntary obedience.

Living my faith

- By serving and loving others I'm going to show God how much I love him.

- At home I'm going to help out my parents with anything they ask of me, even if it's something hard or I don't feel like doing. I'm going to help my brothers and sisters even when they don't ask me.
- At school _____
  _____

- With my friends _____
  _____

Shepherds, Come and See!

The Birth of Jesus
Chapter 1, Lesson 3

Remember

the Archangel Gabriel told Mary she was going to be the Mother of Jesus. She immediately accepted helping God in this mission.

Now you're going to discover

Jesus was born, humble and poor, to save you; and some shepherds were the first to go and adore the Son of God.

In the Gospel we read

"In those days a decree went out from Caesar Augustus that the whole world should be enrolled. This was the first enrollment, when Quirinius was governor of Syria. So all went to be enrolled, each to his own town. And Joseph too went up from Galilee from the town of Nazareth to Judea, to the City of David that is called Bethlehem, because he was of the house and family of David, to be enrolled with Mary, his betrothed, who was with child. While they were there, the time came for her to have her child, and she gave birth to her firstborn son. She wrapped him in swaddling clothes and laid him in a manger, because there was no room for them in the inn. Now there were shepherds in that region living in the fields and keeping the night watch over their flock. The angel of the Lord appeared to them and the glory of the Lord shone around them, and they were struck with great fear. The angel said to them, *'Do not be afraid; for behold, I proclaim to you good news of great joy that will be for all the people. For today in the city of David a savior has been born for you who is Messiah and Lord. And this will be a sign for you: you will find an infant wrapped in swaddling clothes and lying in a manger.'* And suddenly there was a multitude of the heavenly host with the angel, praising God and saying: *'Glory to God in the highest and on earth peace to those on whom his favor rests.'* When the angels went away from them to heaven, the shepherds said to one another, *'Let us go, then, to Bethlehem to see this thing that has taken place, which the Lord has made known to us.'* So they went in haste and found Mary and Joseph, and the infant lying in the manger. When they saw this, they made known the message that had been told them about this child. All who heard it were amazed by what had been told them by the shepherds. And Mary kept all these things, reflecting on them in her heart. Then the shepherds returned, glorifying and praising God for all they had heard and seen, just as it had been told to them. When eight days were completed for his circumcision, he was named Jesus, the name given him by the angel before he was conceived in the womb."

Lk 2: 1-21

If you had to pick where Jesus would be born, what place would you have picked?

Place: _____ Reason: _____

Why do you think Christ was born in a lowly stable? _____

_____

Using the numbers below, write the correct number in each circle on the opposite page.

1 Filled the sky, singing a hymn of glory and praise to God.

2 He put his trust in God, accepting the job of being Jesus' foster father, which he carried out with great love and devotion.

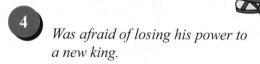

3 Brought words of great joy.

4 Was afraid of losing his power to a new king.

5 Heard the angel's greeting and became the first ones to go to adore the Son of God.

6 His great love for us led him to become a man and be born poor and lowly in a stable.

7 Never imagined that the census he ordered would allow Sacred Scripture to be fulfilled.

8 Followed a heavenly sign in their search for the Savior, certain that they were going to find him.

9 Through her acceptance of God's will, the promise of salvation is fulfilled in her.

 The three Wise men

 Mary

 The angel

 St. Joseph

 The Christ Child

 King Herod

 The choir of angels

 The shepherds

 Caesar Augustus

Answer the questions.

Why did Jesus want to be born in a lowly stable?

_____

What did the angel tell the shepherds?

_____

Why did the shepherds go to the stable?

_____

What did they do when they got there?

_____

What did the shepherds do when they left the stable, after seeing Jesus?

_____

Write a story to match the drawings.

_____

Put on a Christmas play with your friends, showing the birth of Christ. You and your friends will play the part of the Wise Men, each one bringing his own gift for the Christ Child. What will you give Jesus? Why? Remember that the Wise Men gave him the best they had.

The shepherds knew that their God and Savior lay inside the stable, and so they went in with great respect and veneration.

Do you remember the Second Commandment? Write it down here.

The Second Commandment instructs us to respect the name of God and all sacred objects.

Are the children in the pictures below keeping the Second Commandment? Circle "yes" or "no" and then explain why.

This boy is swearing, taking God's name in vain.

Yes

No

Why? _____

_____

These boys are well-behaved in the chapel.

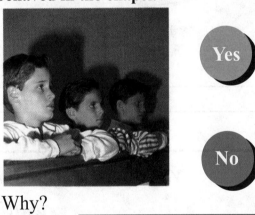

Yes

No

Why? _____

_____

This boy handles sacred objects with great respect.

Yes

No

Why? _____

_____

These boys are playing around in church.

Yes

No

Why? _____

_____

The shepherds went to adore Jesus. You can do the same thing as often as you like. Write a little story to go with these drawings:

_____

_____

You can adore Jesus as often as you like, because he is waiting for you in the

T _ _ _ _ _ _ _ _ _ _ E

Just as the angel told the shepherds about Jesus' birth, inviting them to go to see him, so we too are invited to go adore him in the Tabernacle. The shepherds entered the stable with great respect. How should you act when you enter the chapel or church, where God himself is present?

*When you enter and leave the chapel you should **genuflect** before the Tabernacle, touching the floor with your right knee. This is a sign of **respect and adoration** towards Jesus who is present in the **Eucharist.***

When the priest enters or leaves the chapel you should stand up out of respect. When he speaks you should pay close attention.

*You should observe internal and external **silence.***
***External:** This means not speaking, and whispering if you have to say something. This will help you concentrate better and be more attentive.*
***Internal:** This means not getting distracted by thinking of other things or letting your mind wander. This will help you to adore God, speak with him, and hear what he has to say to you.*

After receiving communion, take a few minutes to give thanks and to adore God with all your heart.

Leave the chapel in an orderly way, without running.

When it's time to go to communion, wait your turn without rushing or bothering those around you.

Fill in the blanks.

Remember always to enter the _____ or church full of _____ because your best _____ and Savior is waiting for you there. And since this great friend of yours is also _____, you should be very _____.

chapel - respectful - God - friend - trust

Don't forget

- To save us, Jesus was born **poor and humble.**
- The angel told the shepherds about the **Savior's** birth. They left everything to go and adore him.
- The Wise Men, full of great **love and respect**, went to **adore Jesus**, offering him the best they had.
- Jesus is our **Savior** and so we, too, should adore him.

Knowing my faith

Why did the Son of God become a man?
He became a man to save us and reconcile us with God.

What is the Second Commandment?
"You shall not take the name of the Lord your God in vain."

What does the Second Commandment instruct us to do?
To respect the name of God and all sacred things.

Living my faith

- God tells me every day that Jesus is with me. I'm going to go to the chapel every day to visit Jesus and to receive him in communion, being sure always to give a good example to others of how we should behave in his presence.
- This week I'm going to offer my daily communion for:

Who are these men?

Wise Men Adore the Newborn King
Chapter 1, Lesson 4

Remember
Jesus was born in a simple stable. Three Wise Men came in search of him.

Now you're going to see some people rejected the infant Jesus, while others welcomed him with joy.

The Gospel tells us

"When Jesus was born in Bethlehem of Judea, in the days of King Herod, behold, magi from the east arrived in Jerusalem, saying, *'Where is the newborn king of the Jews? We saw his star at its rising and have come to do him homage.'* When King Herod heard this, he was greatly troubled, and all Jerusalem with him. Assembling all the chief priests and the scribes of the people, he inquired of them where the Messiah was to be born. They said to him, *'In Bethlehem of Judea, for thus it has been written through the prophet: "And you, Bethlehem, land of Judah, are by no means least among the rulers of Judah; since from you shall come a ruler, who is to shepherd my people Israel."* Then Herod called the magi secretly and ascertained from them the time of the star's appearance. He sent them to Bethlehem and said, *'Go and search diligently for the child. When you have found him, bring me word, that I too may go and do him homage.'* After their audience with the king they set out. And behold, the star that they had seen at its rising preceded them, until it came and stopped over the place where the child was.

"They were overjoyed at seeing the star, and on entering the house they saw the child with Mary his mother. They prostrated themselves and did him homage. Then they opened their treasures and offered him gifts of gold, frankincense, and myrrh. And having been warned in a dream not to return to Herod, they departed for their country by another way."

Mt 2:1-12

Fill in the blanks in the following paragraph, based on what you have just read in the Gospel account.

East - Messiah - Herod - Magi - Jesus - gold - frankincense - star - myrrh - king

The _____ were Wise Men from the _____. They followed a _____ which was to lead them to the_____. When they reached Jerusalem they met with_____, who wanted to know who this new _____ was that they were seeking. The star led the Wise Men to Bethlehem, where they found _____ in a house. They bowed down before him and offered him gifts: _____ because he was a King; _____ because he was Divine; and _____ because he was going to suffer a great deal.

Respond:

Did the Wise Men know where they would find Jesus?

_____

How did they react when they saw the star?

_____

How did they know Jesus was the Savior?

_____

If they themselves were kings, why did they bow down before a newborn babe?

_____

Why was Herod worried when he heard about a newborn king?

_____

What can we learn from the Wise Men's attitude toward Jesus?

_____

"All of Jeruslem grew troubled"

There were no doubt many different reactions among the people living in Jerusalem when they heard about the Wise Men coming in search of the newborn king.

• Some people saw the Wise Men come into town and they saw the star, but paid no attention to either event.
• Others thought the Wise Men were just plain confused.
• Still others asked questions, but weren't really interested.
• There were some who didn't understand what was going on; but, they trust, followed the star, and came upon the Savior.
• Some, like Herod, just got worried.
• Some thought it was too much trouble to go to Bethlehem.

What about you? How would you have reacted?_____

Where is it?

I can't see it because I'm thinking about too many other things.

I've seen it, but I just don't feel like following it.

What am I supposed to do? I don't know how to follow it?

I've seen it, but following it would be too hard!

At Mass, the Holy Spirit awakens my faith, converts my heart, and helps me adhere to God's will, and teaches me how to follow the liturgy.

I pray every day, and that's why I can see it.

Look! There it is! How wonderful!

I found the star in the chapel. I want to follow it.

And I, (name) _____, have I seen the star? _____ Do I want to follow it? _____

What am I going to do to follow it? _____
_____
_____
_____

The **Epiphany** is the revelation of Christ the Savior to all men.

The Wise Men came from distant lands. They were not part of the Jewish people. They came in search of the newborn king of the Jews, to render homage to him who was the King of the Universe and the Savior of all men of good will.

The Wise Men represented all people bowing down before their King and Savior.

For the Wise Men, the star was a sign from God, leading them to him. God sends you signs, too, every day and throughout your entire life: a piece of advice from a friend or teacher, a special book you read, help from your parents, and guidance from your conscience.

What signs from God are you able to find in you life?

Think of an ordinary day in your life and write down the signs you see.

at home	at school	with your friends

"They were overjoyed when they saw the star"

Are you familiar with the lives of the saints? Write down what you know about these saints. If you don't know anything about them, ask your mother to help you find out about them.

St. Francis of Assisi

_____

_____

St. Ignatius of Loyola

_____

_____

St. Clare

_____

_____

St. Teresa of Avila

_____

_____

What do they all have in common?

Finish the sentence using these words: **joy - Christian - Jesus**

Having found _____ *is the great* _____ *of a* _____.

The kings were overjoyed to see the star again, and the saints found joy in knowing that Christ loved them. Joy should also characterize all Christians.

Can you imagine one of the Wise Men going into the stable in Bethlehem sad and depressed?

Can you imagine St. Francis mad or irritated as he told people about his friend Jesus?

Can you imagine the Pope angry or upset as he gives his blessing to some children?

Some things in life make everyone happy, no matter who they are. In addition to these kinds of things, there are others that make Christians immensely happy, **with a happiness no one can take from us.**

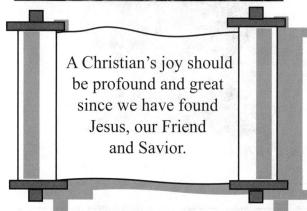

A Christian's joy should be profound and great since we have found Jesus, our Friend and Savior.

Draw a red line under the things that make you and all people happy, and a blue line under the things that make you happy as a Catholic Christian.

- Knowing that God loves me

- Being faithful to Jesus, my best friend

- Having a big house

- Seeing all the gifts God has given me

- Knowing I can receive Jesus in the Eucharist

- Knowing that God will always forgive me in Confession

- Knowing that I'm very smart

- Having a lot of friends

- Trusting that Jesus wants to save me

- Going to lots of parties

- Knowing that I'm invited to heaven

- Winning a prize in a raffle

You can experience great joy finding Jesus, just as the Wise Men did when they found him.

"...on entering the house they saw the child with Mary his mother. They prostrated themselves and did him homage."

The Wise Men went to Bethlehem looking for a Savior. What did they find? An infant with his parents. They didn't turn around and leave, however. They stayed to offer him their gifts, to do him homage, and to contemplate him. No one knows how long they stayed there, contemplating Jesus with deep love and respect, aware that this small baby was the Savior of all men.

You, too, can contemplate Jesus in this way by practicing contemplative prayer. Imagine yourself in the stable, picture Mary taking care of Jesus, Joseph smiling on both of them, the shepherds gathered around.

You can do this whenever you go to the chapel to visit Jesus in the Eucharist, and above all during **Eucharistic Adoration.**

To adore Christ in the Blessed Sacrament is to adore Jesus exactly as the Wise Men and shepherds did. It's a special time when Jesus wants to fill us with many graces.

Eucharistic Adoration is a very special time. A priest exposes the Blessed Sacrament, places it in a monstrance on the altar, and we pray to Jesus, offering him our adoration and praise.

Match up the columns.

1. Contemplative prayer

2. Monstrance

3. Blessed Sacrament

4. Adoration and respect

○ The Eucharist

○ The attitude we should have around the Tabernacle

○ To gaze on Jesus, listen to his words, and silently love him

○ Used for exposing the Blessed Sacrament

Don't forget

- The Wise Men were given a sign to help them find the **Savior.**
- The Wise Men followed the sign and went to **adore** the Savior.
- Salvation is intended for **all people**, though some, like Herod, reject it.
- The greatest joy that we Christians can have is to find Jesus and the salvation he brings to us.
- We can adore Jesus in the **Eucharist.**

Knowing my faith

What is the "Epiphany"?
It was the moment in which Jesus revealed himself to all men.

Is it a good idea to visit Jesus in the Eucharist?
Yes, to thank him and tell him how much we love him.

Living my faith

- Just like the Wise Men, I'm going to go to the chapel to adore Jesus in the Eucharist and to ask him to help me see his signs.

- I'm going to offer Jesus a gift (write it down here):

_____

- Finding Jesus should be a Christian's greatest joy, so I'm going to go to Communion every day. After Communion I'm going to bring Christ to others through my joy and happiness.

The Birth of Christ
Chapter 1
Review

Match up the columns.
Place the number in the correct circle.

1. Was chosen by God to help him save all men...

2. God sent him to Mary as a messenger...

3. Mary responded to God's invitation with...

4. When we pray the Angelus we recall...

5. The cousin Mary went to visit was named...

6. Mary responded to her cousin's greeting with a song called...

7. Jesus was born in a humble...

8. An angel appeared to them and they went to adore Jesus:

9. The Second Commandment instructs us to...

10. The sign that led the Wise Men to the Savior was a...

11. Jesus' revelation as the Savior of all men is known as the...

12. We can adore Christ as the Wise Men did thanks to the...

○ Elizabeth

○ The Annunciation

○ stable

○ Mary

○ the Magnificat

○ the shepherds

○ respect God's name

○ star

○ humility and obedience

○ the Archangel Gabriel

○ Epiphany

○ Eucharist

Study the following words:

Humility. Visitation. Servant. Nativity. Adoration.

Now fill in the missing letters:

__ umility. V __ s __ tat __ on. Ser __ ant. Na __ ivi __ y. __ dor __ tion.

Christ's Infancy

Chapter 2

The Presentation in the Temple
Chapter 2, Lesson 1

Remember
God is the one who has given you everything you have.
Now you're going to discover
all you'll receive by going to church, and what you'll lose if you don't go.

The Gospel tells us
"When the days were completed for their purification according to the law of Moses, they took him up to Jerusalem to present him to the Lord, just as it is written in the law of the Lord, 'Every male that opens the womb shall be consecrated to the Lord,' and to offer the sacrifice of 'a pair of turtledoves or two young pigeons,' in accordance with the dictate in the law of the Lord. Now there was a man in Jerusalem whose name was Simeon. This man was righteous and devout, awaiting the consolation of Israel, and the Holy Spirit was upon him. It had been revealed to him by the Holy Spirit that he should not see death before he had seen the Messiah of the Lord. He came in the Spirit into the temple; and when the parents brought in the child Jesus to perform the custom of the law in regard to him, he took him into his arms and blessed God, saying: 'Now, Master, you may let your servant go in peace, according to your word, for my eyes have seen your salvation...' There was also a prophetess, Anna, the daughter of Phanuel, of the tribe of Asher. She was advanced in years, having lived seven years with her husband after her marriage, and then as a widow until she was eighty-four. She never left the temple, but worshipped night and day with fasting and prayer. And coming forward at that very time, she gave thanks to God and spoke about the child to all who were awaiting the redemption of Jerusalem."

Lk 2:22-29; 36-38

Those who were there

Mary

- She knew better than anyone that Jesus belonged to God, and she went to the temple full of joy to offer her son to God.
- She was sought to fulfill all God's wishes and to fulfill them to the last detail; at the precise moment assigned by the Law; and according to its prescriptions, offering a pair of turtledoves or pigeons.

Joseph
- The head of the family, he takes Mary and Jesus to Jerusalem and provides them with everything necessary for the ceremony.

The Prophetess Anna

- She belonged to a prominent family in Jerusalem, and could have spent all her time attending the social functions. She chose instead to remain in the temple day and night, serving God through prayer and fasting.
- She knew God alone could make her truly happy, and that's why she chose to spend all her time in the temple.
- When Mary and Joseph brought Jesus to the temple, Anna was there and was able to see him and adore him. For almost eighty years she had gone to the temple every day, but if she had failed to go just that one day, she would have missed the chance to see Jesus.
- Anna praised God out loud and spoke about Jesus to all those who awaited the salvation of Israel.

Jesus

- Small and defenseless, he places himself in the hands of his parents, going wherever they take him. A mere infant, he fulfills the Law even though he is not aware of it at the time.

Simeon

- A just and upright man, that is, he lived in perfect obedience to God's commandments so as to be at peace with God when the Messiah arrived.
- He knew he would see the Messiah before dying and used to go to the temple every day, longing for that moment to arrive.

- He saw the infant Jesus and realized that he was the one he was waiting to see. Unable to contain his joy, he ran to Jesus and clasped him in his arms. How lucky Simeon was!

Match up each figure of the Gospel account with the behavior that best represents him or her.

Who am I like?

ANNA

SIMEON

JOSEPH

I realize I belong to God since he has given me everything I have and am, I offer to God everything I do, and I happily keep the Ten Commandments.

I obey my parents (even though I might not always understand their reasons) because I know they are more familiar than I with the laws of God, and I look to them to help me carry out what God asks of me.

I am a leader and guide for my family, sharing with them what I know about God and inspiring them by providing them with good example in keeping God's Commandments.

I realize I am much luckier than this person because I can have Jesus far closer to me than just holding him in my arms; when I receive him in Communion I can embrace him in my heart, with all my love, and I can show him how much I love him with every one of my actions.

I never miss Mass on Sunday because I don't want to miss anything important God might have in store for me. I know that God is the only one who can make me truly happy, so going to Mass is much more important than any television show, sports event, or time spent at a friend's house.

JESUS

MARY

The Third Commandment instructs us to "keep holy the Sabbath." This means we should make Sunday a holy day by resting and serving God, thanking him for all he has given us.

Fill in the blanks below by using the words from the boxes.

dedicating	Creator	waiting	God	others	only

Sunday	Communion	Commandments	Third	know	church

- God is my _____.
- _____ has given me everything I have and am.
- I belong to God and so I dedicate every _____ to him and go to church.
- God gave us the Ten _____ as an instruction manual for being happy.
- The _____ Commandment tells us to keep Sundays holy.
- Keeping Sunday holy means _____ it to God.
- God is the _____ one who can make me perfectly happy.
- When I go to _____ I meet Jesus himself in person.
- Christ is _____ for me at Mass and has important things to say to me.
- When I receive _____ I embrace Jesus in my heart.
- At Mass I come to _____ Jesus very deeply.
- I need to get to know Jesus so that I can then teach _____ about him.

Draw a circle around the things that can be done on Sundays, in keeping with the Third Commandment. Cross out the things that shouldn't be done.

- Attend Mass
- Go to work
- Visit my grandparents

- Play sports
- Visit someone who is ill
- Spend time with my family

- Relax like
- Read a good book
- Do something God doesn't

- Go to a state park
- Forget about God
- See a good movie

Witnessing a miracle in action: Holy Mass

Now we're going to learn about each part of the Mass so that we can understand it better and participate in it just as God wants. The Mass has two main parts: The Liturgy of the Word and the Liturgy of the Eucharist.

LITURGY OF THE WORD

It is divided into three parts: the Readings, the Homily, and the Prayers of the Faithful.

1. The Readings We listen and get to know the Word of God. There are three readings, besides the Responsorial Psalm which comes between the first and second readings:

- **First Reading**
It is taken from the Old Testament or from the Acts of the Apostles and helps us to understand better many things that Jesus did. We remain seated during this reading. Right after the first reading comes the Responsorial Psalm, taken from the Psalms of David. Through it we give praise to God.

- **Second Reading**
This is from the New Testament, either the Acts of the Apostles or the letters written by the first apostles. The second reading helps us to understand how the first Christians lived and preached Christ to others. This helps us, too, to understand better what Christ teaches us. The second reading also helps us to understand the Church's traditions. We remain seated for this reading. It is followed by the Alleluia, which is a short song of praise that reminds us of the Resurrection.

- **The Gospel**
This reading is taken from one of the four Gospels, depending on the liturgical cycle. In it we hear about the life and teachings of Jesus. This is where we can get to know Jesus first-hand: the things he felt and did, the things he taught and showed us. We stand up during this reading, which is done by a priest or deacon.

2. THE HOMILY

Here the priest helps us to understand what the three readings mean, and especially how to put them into practice in our lives. We sit down for the homily. Sometimes we can't understand what the priest is saying, either because we can't hear him well enough or because he uses words and ideas we don't understand very well yet at our age. We shouldn't let our minds wander when this happens. We can use the time to re-read the readings, to reflect on them, to pray within ourselves and ask God what he wants to teach us through them.

3. THE PRAYER OF THE FAITHFUL

We stand up for this and unite ourselves to everyone at Mass in order to pray to God together for the things that concern us all: the Pope, the sick, the poor, the dying and recently deceased, etc. We should also use this time to ask God interiorly for the things we most need. This prayer brings the Liturgy of the Word to an end.

LITURGY OF THE EUCHARIST

The Liturgy of the Eucharist is divided into three parts:

1. OFFERTORY

Here the gifts of bread and wine are taken to the altar and the priest offers them to God so that they can become the body and blood of Christ. We should make the most of this part of the Mass to offer to God our lives, our resolutions, our prayer concerns, our love for him, and our talents. We should ask him to bless all these things and to use them for the good of the Church. This is also the time when we should promise God to make a renewed effort to reach our human and spiritual goals. During the offertory we remain seated.

2. CONSECRATION

This is the most solemn part of the Mass, the moment when the bread and wine really and truly become the Body and Blood of Jesus. God comes among us so we can draw near to him in a mystery of marvelous love and contemplate him with the greatest respect and devotion. We should use these few moments to adore God in the Eucharist. It's not very often we have someone so important right in front of us.
During the Consecration we kneel down with an attitude of adoration.

3. COMMUNION

The word means "common union," or "union together." When we go to Communion we not only receive Jesus and embrace him with love and joy like Simeon, but we also unite ourselves to the entire Church to all Catholic Christians in this same love and joy. We should never pass up the chance to go to Communion. To receive Communion we kneel down or receive it standing, bowing our head slightly as a sign of respect.

The following alphabet soup contains names of people who participated in Jesus' Presentation in the Temple. It also contains the parts of the Mass. Find the words.

L	I	T	U	R	G	Y	O	F	T	H	E	W	O	R	D	O	E	A	Q
B	A	B	S	T	R	T	T	E	Q	W	I	U	R	G	G	M	A	Z	A
K	F	I	R	S	T	R	E	A	D	I	N	G	P	A	M	E	N	O	N
G	Y	E	T	A	K	O	I	P	N	M	S	A	N	N	A	I	T	A	V
O	Q	Y	P	F	S	I	M	E	O	N	I	P	E	T	O	E	C	E	S
S	I	P	A	T	U	O	L	I	C	E	A	Q	W	Z	G	M	I	C	A
P	A	T	H	J	O	S	E	P	H	O	M	I	L	Y	O	R	R	I	T
E	K	A	O	Y	O	F	F	E	R	T	O	R	Y	M	E	O	N	O	Q
L	P	E	M	A	R	Y	P	E	N	J	E	S	U	S	Q	I	E	R	E
I	C	O	N	S	E	C	R	A	T	I	O	N	A	M	E	C	A	M	I
T	P	R	A	Y	E	R	O	F	T	H	E	F	A	I	T	H	F	U	L
U	C	O	M	M	U	N	I	O	N	P	O	M	E	R	O	S	T	Q	Z
R	S	E	C	O	N	D	R	E	A	D	I	N	G	A	B	I	C	O	C
G	Q	S	Z	U	T	V	P	U	R	P	L	O	N	G	A	T	E	N	B
Y	O	F	T	H	E	E	U	C	H	A	R	I	S	T	R	A	S	T	A

1. Liturgy of the Word
2. First Reading
3. Second Reading
4. Gospel
5. Homily
6. Prayer of the Faithfu
7. Liturgy of the Eucharist
8. Offertory
9. Consecration
10. Communion
11. Joseph
12. Mary
13. Jesus
14. Anna
15. Sime

Connect the three columns with lines.

PARTS OF THE MASS	POSITION	MEANING
First reading	•seated	• We receive Jesus into our hearts.
Second reading		• The priest explains the readings.
Gospel	•standing	• Generally from the Old Testament.
Homily		• The priest offers the bread and wine.
Prayer of the faithful	•kneeling	• The bread and wine become the body and blood of Christ.
Offertory		• A passage from the life of Jesus.
Consecration	•Walking	• A reading from the New Testament.
Communion		• We pray for the Church's needs.

Group Activity

1. What law did Mary and Joseph obey when they brought Jesus to the temple?

2. Why do we say that we belong to God?

3. Why was Simeon so happy to see Jesus?

4. Why did Anna prefer to spend her time in the temple rather than some place else?

5. Give three reasons to explain why going to Mass is a good thing.

6. Explain how to live the Third Commandment, "Keep holy the Sabbath?"

Don't forget

The parts of the Mass:

MASS
- LITURGY OF THE WORD
  - FIRST READING
  - RESPONSORIAL PSALM
  - SECOND READING
  - ALLELUIA
  - GOSPEL
  - HOMILY
  - PRAYER OF THE FAITHFUL
- LITURGY OF THE EUCHARIST
  - OFFERTORY
  - CONSECRATION
  - COMMUNION

Knowing my faith

What is the Third Commandment?
"You shall keep holy the Sabbath day."

What does it mean to keep holy the Sabbath, or the religious feastdays?
It means that we should dedicate Sundays and holy days to resting, serving, and worshipping God, praying, and living out Christ's commandment of love.

Why should we keep Sundays and feastdays holy?
Because we need to rest and because we need to thank God for all that he has given us.

What does "Holy day of obligation" mean?
It refers to days on which we must attend Mass.

Living my faith

When I go to Mass on Sunday I will do my best to:
• Arrive on time; take on the appropriate postures; participate in all the prayers by responding out loud; carefully follow the readings, either using the missalette or listening to the lector; pay attention to the homily; remain attentive and devout throughout the Mass; receive Communion; pray in silence after Communion; wait until Mass is completely over to leave.

• I'm going to draw up a program with my family to help us keep Sundays holy by going to Mass, resting, and making the most of each Sunday to perform some good deed, such as visiting a sick relative.

Herod was Furious!

The Flight into Egypt
Chapter 2, Lesson 2

Remember
how Herod was afraid that Jesus would take his place as king of the Jews? Herod told the Wise Men to come back and tell him where the newborn king was to be found, but they didn't.

Now you're going to see
God sends you messengers to point out the path you need to follow.

The Gospel tells us

"When they had departed, behold, the angel of the Lord appeared to Joseph in a dream and said, *'Rise, take the child and his mother, flee to Egypt, and stay there until I tell you. Herod is going to search for the child to destroy him.'* Joseph rose and took the child and his mother by night and departed for Egypt. He stayed there until the death of Herod, that what the Lord had said through the prophet might be fulfilled, *'Out of Egypt I called my son.'* When Herod realized that he had been deceived by the magi, he became furious. He ordered the massacre of all the boys in Bethlehem and its vicinity two years old and under, in accordance with the time he had ascertained from the magi. Then was fulfilled what had been said through Jeremiah the prophet: *'A voice was heard in Ramah, sobbing and loud lamentation; Rachel weeping for her children, and she would not be consoled, since they were no more.'* When Herod had died, behold, the angel of the Lord appeared in a dream to Joseph in Egypt and said, *'Rise, take the child and his mother and go to the land of Israel, for those who sought the child's life are dead.'* He rose, took the child and his mother, and went to the land of Israel. But when he heard that Archelaus was ruling over Judea in place of his father Herod, he was afraid to go back there. And because he had been warned in a dream, he departed for the region of Galilee. He went and dwelt in a town called Nazareth, so that what had been spoken through the prophets might be fulfilled, *'He shall be called a Nazorean.'*

Mt 2: 13-23

Find the correct answer and underline it.

1. How did Joseph react to the angel's message?

a) He doubted whether it was true and went back to sleep.
b) He followed the angel's instructions.
c) He got upset because it meant changing his plans.
d) He got mad at Mary for bringing such problems on him.

2. In what way did Joseph obey?

a) He grumbled for a bit and then obeyed.
b) He complained to God saying, "Why me? Let Mary and her son go to Egypt on their own!"
c) He bargained with the angel saying, "Okay, I'll go. Just tell God that he better provide me with a house and work in Egypt!"
d) He got up then and there and obeyed with full trust.

If you could have spoken with Herod before the massacre of the children, what would you have said to him to get him to think things over again and change his mind?

_____
_____
_____
_____

Color in the line that connects the angel with the true reason God sent him to Joseph.

He wanted to punish Herod by ruining his plans.

He wanted Jesus to see the Pyramids of Egypt.

He saw that his Son Jesus was in danger and wanted to save him.

The angel told God he wanted to visit earth.

What do we know about angels?

Angels are spiritual beings created by God. Endowed with intelligence and will, their mission is to glorify God and to help us live according to God's will.

God knows very well that throughout our lives we face spiritual and bodily dangers, and so he has assigned each one of us an angel to guide us and watch over us. We call such angels **Guardian Angels**. We can't see them because they're spiritual beings, but they are always at our side helping us and looking out for us.

God's plan is not always clear to us

Mary and Joseph thought Jesus would be born in Nazareth, where they lived. They had to go to Bethlehem because of the census ordered by Caesar Augustus. When Jesus was born there, they thought they would stay there for a time, and suddenly God sent them to Egypt. God's plans for us can sometimes be very different from our own plans. As our wise and loving Father, he always knows what's best for us. He wants us to be happy with him forever, even though it may mean giving up some things for now.

To let us know his will for us, and to help us carry it out, he sends us **"messages"** (such as Caesar's edict) or **"messengers"** (such as the angel).

Study these examples

Your friend Steve wants to go with his friends to see the movie "Blood Bath II." God, however, wants Steve to use his time well so that he can be a better person. Steve's mother won't let him go to the movies because they need to go and visit their sick grandmother.
God's message: It's better to visit your grandma than to waste your time watching bad movies.
Messenger: Steve's mother.

Your cousin Alice talks badly about everyone, except her favorite friend, Judy. God wants Alice to learn to see the good in all people. Judy tells Alice not to be so critical of others.
God's message: We shouldn't speak badly of others.
Messenger: Alice's friend.

Mary no doubt would have preferred to have Jesus born at home in Nazareth without any complications. God wanted to teach us the value of poverty through Jesus' birth. Caesar's edict was issued and Mary and Joseph had to go to Bethlehem. Jesus was born in a stable.
God's message: Mary and Joseph should go to Bethlehem to register.
Messenger: Caesar Augustus.

Find God's messages and messengers in these examples.

Ricardo has everything it takes to be a great baseball player. He thinks he's already good enough and never goes to practice because it's hard work. God wants Ricardo to become the very best he can. This year the coach didn't let Ricardo play on the team and he became very sad.

Message:_____

Messenger:_____

Caroline is very smart. She learns very quickly, but she's very shy and hates to appear in public. God wants Caroline to overcome her shyness so that she can use her intelligence to teach others what she has learned. Caroline's drama teacher picks her for the leading role in the school play.

Message:_____

Messenger:_____

Divine Providence

Divine Providence refers to all the things that God, in his wisdom and love, allows in our life to help us get to heaven. We need to embrace all these things full of trust in our Heavenly Father.

The things God allows in his Divine Providence don't always agree with what we would prefer. Why?

Study this example.
Andrew is two years old. One day it gets cold in the house and so Andrew's father lights a fire in the fireplace. Andrew is fascinated by the colors of the fire and wants to touch it. His father won't let him get close to it and Andrew complains and won't stop crying.

Read the following questions and when your teacher calls on you tell the class how you would answer them.
Did Andrew's father do the right thing in not letting him get too close to the fire? Why did the father act that way? Did Andrew understand? Would Andrew have been happier sticking his hand in the fire?

After studying this example, can you answer the question: Why are the things that God wants sometimes different from the things I want?

The importance of always doing God's will?

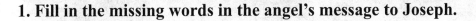

Exercise

1. Fill in the missing words in the angel's message to Joseph.

'Rise, take the _____ and his mother, flee to _____, and stay there until I tell you. _____ is going to search for the child to _____ him.'

2. What would have happened if Joseph had ignored the message God sent him?

_____

How can I know God's will?

1. By asking him in prayer.

2. By listening to the "messengers" he sends me:

- my parents
- my teachers
- those who have authority over me
- those who ask my help

3. By reflecting on the "messages" he sends me:

- his Commandments
- the rules my parents have made at home
- the rules I've been given at school
- the things that happen to me that I haven't planned

4. Asking my Guardian Angel to guide and enlighten me.

Learn this prayer to your Guardian Angel:

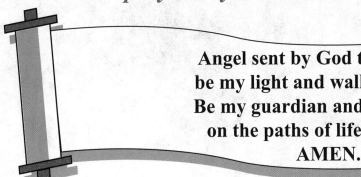

**Angel sent by God to guide me,
be my light and walk beside me.
Be my guardian and protect me,
on the paths of life direct me.
AMEN.**

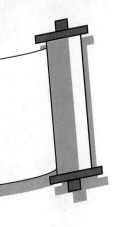

Don't forget

• Herod, overcome by fear and envy, wanted to kill Jesus.
• God sent an angel to Joseph to tell him about Herod's intentions.
• Joseph obeyed and fled to Egypt.
• By his obedience Joseph saved Jesus' life.
• God's plans are not always our plans.
• God lets us know his plans through his Divine Providence and through the people and events in our lives.
• God has given each of us a Guardian Angel to guide us through life.

Knowing my faith

What is "Divine Providence"?
"Divine Providence" refers to things God allows to help us get to heaven.

What kind of attitude should we have towards Divine Providence?
We should embrace it, full of trust in our Heavenly Father.

What are angels?
They are spiritual beings created by God and endowed with intelligence and will.

What mission do the angels have?
To glorify God and help us to live according to God's will.

What is a "Guardian Angel"?
It is the angel God has assigned to each one of us to help us, guide us, and protect us from bodily and spiritual dangers.

Living my faith

• I'm going to make a special effort to discern the messages God sends me every day through his Divine Providence.
• I'm going to follow the rules I've been given at home and at school, aware that they are messages God sends me through my parents and teachers.
• I'm going to write down the prayer to the Guardian Angel and pray it every morning.

Jesus is lost!

Jesus is found in the temple
Chapter 2, Lesson 3

Remember
**Jesus went up to Jerusalem every year
with his family for the Passover.**

*Now you're going to find
out about*
**the duties your parents
have towards you!**

The Gospel tells us

"Each year his parents went to Jerusalem for the feast of Passover, and when he was twelve years old, they went up according to festival custom. After they had completed its days, as they were returning, the boy Jesus remained behind in Jerusalem, but his parents did not know it. Thinking that he was in the caravan, they journeyed for a day and looked for him among their relatives and acquaintances, but not finding him, they returned to Jerusalem to look for him. After three days they found him in the temple, sitting in the midst of the teachers, listening to them and asking them questions, and all who heard him were astounded at his understanding and his answers. When his parents saw him, they were astonished, and his mother said to him, *'Son, why have you done this to us? Your father and I have been looking for you with great anxiety.'* And he said to them, *'Why were you looking for me? Did you not know that I must be in my Father's house?'* But they did not understand what he said to them."

Lk 2:41-50

Exercise

Circle the correct word to fill in the blank.

1. When Joseph and Mary realized Jesus was not in the caravan, they became _____ and went to look for him.

angry   **worried**   **happy**   **curious**

2. Joseph and Mary _____ _____ about anything that might happen to Jesus.

didn't care   **got mad**   **were concerned**   **didn't think**

3. Mary and Joseph knew that God had entrusted Jesus to them so that they would _____ _____ _____ _____ him.

lose   **crucify**   **care for and rear**   **forgive**

4. Jesus _____ God's will for him.

ignored   **hated**   **knew**   **questioned**

5. Jesus didn't disobey his parents, he knew his mission called him to _____ _____ _____.

get Mary worried   **fulfill God's will**   **get lost in the temple**   **please Mary**

Fill in the missing words.

...his mother said to him, 'Son, why have you done this to us? Your _____ and I have been looking for you with great anxiety.' And he said to them, 'Why were you looking for me? Did you not know that I _____ be in my _____ house?' But they did not understand what he said to them.

Activity

Help Joseph and Mary find Jesus

Find these people too:

Joseph / Mary / A Levite collecting taxes from a poor widow / A Roman soldier tossing a stone / A Pharisee praying in public / A sheep being taken to sacrifice / A blind man begging for alms

God does not leave me on my own

God chose Mary to be Jesus' mother, and Joseph to take care of him as his father on earth. In the same way, God chose your father and mother for you, to help you get to heaven.

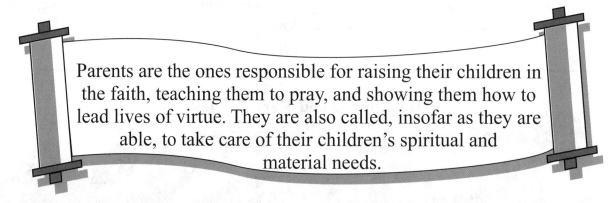

Parents are the ones responsible for raising their children in the faith, teaching them to pray, and showing them how to lead lives of virtue. They are also called, insofar as they are able, to take care of their children's spiritual and material needs.

Match the duties with their correct meanings.

THE DUTIES OF PARENTS

- Raise their children in the faith

- Teach their children to pray

- Teach their children virtue

- "insofar as they are able"

- Take care of their material needs

- Take care of their spiritual needs

THIS MEANS...

- Striving to give their children what they need, according to the financial circumstances of the family. It doesn't mean giving their children everything they want, but rather what they really need.

- Teaching their children to know God and love him.

- Giving their children a home, food, and clothing.

- Teaching their children to be honest, fair, respectful, etc.

- Encouraging, advising, and consoling their children.

- Teaching their children to build a relationship with God.

Check off the things your parents have done for you.

- ☐ Taken care of me ever since I was a baby.
- ☐ Taken me to the doctor when I was sick.
- ☐ Fed me so that I could grow up healthy and strong.
- ☐ Showed concern when something bad happened to me.
- ☐ Taught me to know and love God.
- ☐ Worked to have money to give me the things I need.
- ☐ Taught me to pray.
- ☐ Corrected me when I did something wrong.
- ☐ Helped me to make the right decision in something important.
- ☐ Consoled me when I was sad about something.
- ☐ Cheered me up when I was feeling down.
- ☐ Helped me to be honest, respectful, and polite.
- ☐ Sent me to school so that I could learn.

Complete the list by writing down three other things your parents have done to help you:

1. _____
2. _____
3. _____

Draw a picture of your mother or father doing something good for you.

Don't forget

- Joseph and Mary felt responsible for anything that could happen to Jesus, since God had entrusted him to them to watch over as their own son. That's why they grew worried and went in search of Jesus.
- Jesus knew God's plan for him, and he also knew that carrying it out was the most important thing in his life.
- God has not left me on my own, he has given me my parents to take care of me and guide me on my way to Heaven.

Knowing my faith

What are the duties parents have towards their children?
Parents are responsible for raising their children in the faith and teaching them to pray and live virtuously; they are also responsible for taking care of their children's spiritual and material needs, insofar as they are able.

What is the first school of prayer?
The Christian family is the first school of prayer.

Living my faith

Write a letter thanking your parents for all they've done for you.

Dear Mother and Father,

_____

_____

_____

From your son/daughter who loves you,

Just the opposite!

The Holy Family
Chapter 2, Lesson 4

Remember
**The Fourth Commandment instructs us to
"Honor your father and mother."**

Now you're going to discover
You have only four duties towards your parents.

The Gospel tells us

"He went down with them and came to Nazareth, and was obedient to them; and his mother kept all these things in her heart. And Jesus advanced in wisdom and age and favor before God and man."

Lk 2: 51-52

Exercise

What do these phrases from the Gospel refer to? Match each one up with its meaning.

"...and was obedient to them..."

• Jesus was kind and respectful towards all.

"...Jesus advanced in wisdom..."

• Jesus studied to learn more every day.

"...Jesus advanced in age..."

• Jesus obeyed his parents, trusted in them, helped them, and loved them.

"...Jesus advanced in favor before God..."

• Jesus ate right, exercised, and took care of his body to grow up healthy and strong.

"...Jesus advanced in favor before men..."

• Jesus prayed, building a loving relationship. with his Heavenly Father

Who was the most important person in the Holy Family?

• Jesus is God.
• Mary was chosen by God to be the Mother of the Redeemer.
• Joseph was a just man who carried out all that God asked of him.

Write the name of Joseph, Mary, or Jesus, depending on how important they really were.

_____ was the most important.

_____ was the second most important.

_____ was third in importance.

Despite this, Joseph was in charge of the Holy Family. Mary obeyed him, and Jesus obeyed them both. Just the opposite of their order of importance!

By his example Jesus taught us how important it is to obey our parents. Although he was God himself, all-powerful and all-knowing, he obeyed his human parents.

What was it like being part of the Holy Family?

• God wanted Jesus to be born into a family so that he would have someone to take care of him, protect him, help him, and accept him just as he was.

• Mary and Joseph took good care of Jesus. They struggled and worked hard so he wouldn't lack anything, just as all good parents do for their children.

• Joseph was a carpenter, and Jesus helped him in his work. Later on they called Jesus "the carpenter's son."

• Mary made sure their home in Nazareth had everything it needed. Back then, boys used to help their mothers by grinding grain and carrying water from the local well; they helped their fathers in whatever work they did. There's no reason to think Jesus acted any differently. He learned to work hard and to do all he could to help his family.

Nazareth the place where he grew up

Nazareth was a forgotten village in the region of Galilee. It stood a long way away from the *Sea Road*, an important trading route that ran from Damascus to South Palestine. Moreover, it seems there weren't even any roads connecting Nazareth to the rest of Israel. Archeologists have discovered tombs proving that Nazareth was inhabited for at least three hundred years before Jesus' birth. Yet not a single historian of the time mentions it. It was located in a region called "Galilee of the Gentiles," which may mean there were no other Jewish villages in the area. Thus God chose the most remote and hidden place in the world to live most of his years on earth, some thirty years in all.

> **Write a brief composition entitled "A day in the life of Nazareth" and describe what life there was like.**

Does my family have anything in common with Jesus' family?

Fill in this family tree for your family, writing the correct name in each box.

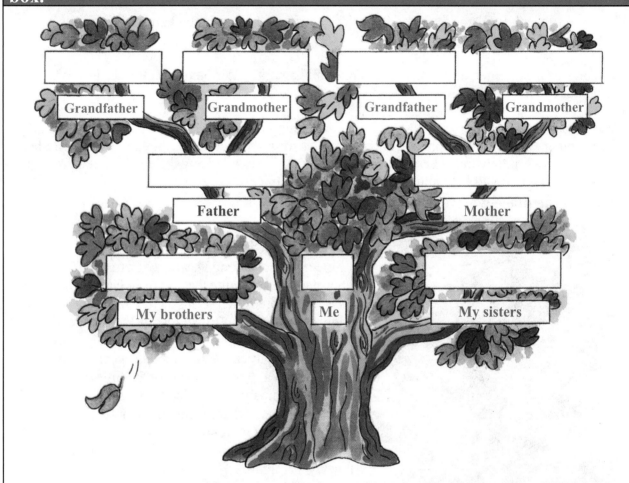

Grandfather	Grandmother	Grandfather	Grandmother

Father

Mother

My brothers

Me

My sisters

- *God wanted me to be born into a family.*
- *God chose special parents just for me.*
- *My parents do for me just what Joseph and Mary did for Jesus.*
- *God wants my family to be like the Holy Family, a place where everyone loves and helps each other.*
- *God wants me to be like Jesus, he wants me to love my parents, respect them, trust them, and obey them.*

Draw a picture of yourself showing that you love, respect, obey, and help your parents.

Do you remember the Fourth Commandment?
Fill in the missing words.

The Fourth Commandment is:
"You shall _____ your father and your _____"

We should honor and respect our parents because they have given us our life and our Christian upbringing. We owe our parents respect, gratitude, and fair obedience. When they grow old or become ill, we owe them our material and moral support.

Children's duties towards their parents:
• *Respect*
• *Gratitude*
• *Fair obedience*
• *Material and moral support in old age and illness*

St. Paul wrote to the Ephesians: "Children, obey your parents, for it is right that you should. 'Honor your father and mother' is the first commandment with a promise attached, in the words: 'that it will be well with you and that you may live long in the land' " (Eph. 6:1-3).

According to St. Paul, what reward will you receive for honoring your parents?

_____
_____
_____
_____

Group Activity

Divide up into three groups. Each group, on its own, should come up with something that can be done to fulfill each of the four duties we have towards our parents. The group should also come up with something that should *not* be done. After each group has finished, the results will be read aloud and everyone should write them down in their own books.

Respect

I should:
Example: *"...speak to my parents in a kind and respectful tone of voice."*
Group 1_____
       2_____
       3_____

I should not:
Example " *...interrupt mother or father when they are speaking."*
Group 1_____
       2_____
       3_____

Gratitude

I should:
Example   *"...go to greet my father with joy when he comes home from work."*
Group 1_____
       2_____
       3_____

I should not:
Example " *...neglect to take care of the books and toys they have given me."*
Group 1_____
       2_____
       3_____

Fair Obedience

I should:
Example *"...cheerfully obey my mother when she tells me to do my homework."*
Group *1* _____
   2 _____
   3 _____

I should not:
Example *"...pretend not to hear when my mother asks me to do something."*
Group *1* _____
   2 _____
   3 _____

Material and moral support in old age and illness

I should:
Example *"...be patient when my mother has to use a walker."*
Group *1* _____
   2 _____
   3 _____

I should not:
Example *"...be mad at my father because at times he forgets things."*
Group *1* _____
   2 _____
   3 _____

Don't forget

- God wanted Jesus to be born into a family so that he would have someone to take care of him, protect him, help him and accept him just as he was.
- By his example, Jesus wanted to teach us how important it is for us to obey our parents. Although he was all-powerful and all-knowing, Jesus obeyed his earthly parents.
- God wanted me to be born into a family, and chose special parents just for me.
- God wants my family to be like the Holy Family, a place where everyone loves and helps each other.
- God wants me to be like Jesus, loving my parents, respecting them, trusting them, and obeying them.

Knowing my faith

What does the Fourth Commandment instruct us to do?
To honor and respect our parents.

Why should we honor and respect our parents?
Because they gave us our life and our Christian upbringing.

What are a child's duties towards his or her parents?
He or she should show them respect, gratitude, and fair obedience, as well as material and moral support in old age and illness.

Living my faith

- I'm going to pick three things from the list we made as a class, and I'm going to put them into practice this week.
- I'm going to talk to my brothers and sisters about ways we can all together show our love for mother and father through our respect and obedience.

Christ's infancy
Chapter 2
Review

Match up the two columns:

1. Mass is divided into two main parts:

2. The correct posture during the consecration:

3. Sundays should be dedicated to...

4. Herod wanted to kill Jesus...

5. Helps us to know God's will for us:

6. The guide God has assigned me is:

7. A child's duty towards his parents is:

8. Jesus grew up in...

9. Jesus was born into a family, and thus taught us the importance of...

10. Jesus was lost in the...

11. Parents' duties towards their children is:

12. This is the first school of prayer:

○ My Guardian Angel

○ Divine Providence

○ respect, gratitude, and obedience

○ out of fear and envy

○ kneeling

○ Liturgy of the Word and Liturgy of the Eucharist

○ Nazareth

○ resting and serving God

○ to raise them well and attend to their needs

○ to obey them

○ the family

○ temple in Jerusalem

Study the following words.

First born; Anna the prophetess; Homily; Providence; Nazareth; Obey; Virtue; Prayer

Fill in the missing letters:

__ ir __ t b __ rn; __ nn __ the __ ro __ h __ t __ ss; Ho __ ily; Pro__iden__e;

N __ z __ r __ th; O __ e __; V __ r __ u __; P __ aye __

The Parables of the Kingdom

Chapter 3

A Sower Went Out to Sow...

The Parable of the Sower
Chapter 3, Lesson 1

Remember

Jesus used parables to teach those who listened to him about the Kingdom of God? Thus he was able to capture their attention and make things understandable for both the simple and the learned. A parable is a story that explains complex things in simple terms by using comparisons.

Now you'll see
if you really want to, you can become like Jesus.

The Gospel tells us

"On that day, Jesus went out of the house and sat down by the sea. Such large crowds gathered around him that he got into a boat and sat down, and the whole crowd stood along the shore. And he spoke to them at length in parables, saying: *'A sower went out to sow. And as he sowed, some seed fell on the path, and birds came and ate it up. Some fell on rocky ground, where it had little soil. It sprang up at once because the soil was not deep, and when the sun rose it was scorched, and it withered for lack of roots. Some seed fell among thorns, and the thorns grew up and choked it. But some seed fell on good soil, and produced fruit, a hundred- or sixty- or thirtyfold. Whoever has ears ought to hear.'*

"*'Hear then the parable of the sower. The seed sown on the path is the one who hears the word of the kingdom without understanding it, and the evil one comes and steals away what was sown in his heart. The seed sown on rocky ground is the one who hears the word and receives it at once with joy. But he has no root and lasts only for a time. When some tribulation or persecution comes because of the word, he immediately falls away. The seed sown among thorns is the one who hears the word, but then worldly anxiety and the lure of riches choke the word and it bears no fruit. But the seed sown on rich soil is the one who hears the word and understands it, who indeed bears fruit and yields a hundred- or sixty- or thirtyfold'.*"

Mt 13:1-9; 18-23

What kind of soil am I?

Match up the two columns with a line:

Rocky soil

• I listen to the Gospel but it doesn't make any sense to me and I don't care; I quickly forget about it.

Soil at the edge of the path

• I like what the Gospel has to say, but I'm afraid others will make fun of me if I take it seriously. I grow afraid and forget all my good resolutions.

Good soil

• I know that what Jesus tells me is good and right, but I'd rather spend my time on things that are more fun or more "important."

Soil covered with thorns

• I pay attention to what Jesus says to me and realize what it means. I know it's the best thing for me and I do everything I can to put it into practice.

What do I consider most important?

There are a lot of good things you can do, but some are more important than others.

Study this list of desirable things.

a) people like me and speak well of me
b) a nice house, nice clothes, and good toys
c) good food and restful sleep
d) be attractive: clean, well-groomed and well-dressed
e) learn lots of new things and know more than others
f) obey and help my parents
g) Know Jesus and his will for me
h) Play and have lots of fun
i) Help others

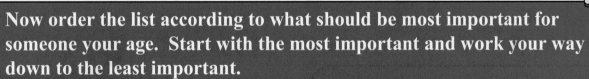

Now order the list according to what should be most important for someone your age. Start with the most important and work your way down to the least important.

Most Important:

1. _____
2. _____
3. _____
4. _____
5. _____
6. _____
7. _____
8. _____

Least Important: 9. _____

This is called having a **"hierarchy of values."**

Soil on the edge of the path

"I'm not interested."
I'm a superficial person. What matters most to me is: "having a good time", playing, having fun, eating what I like, and sleeping as much as I want, never having to put up with any hardship.

Rocky soil

"I'd love to do it, but it's hard and I'll be criticized." What matters most to me is what others have to say about me: looking good, having people like me and speak well of me.

Soil with thorny plants

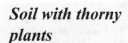

"I make good resolutions, but I fail to carry them out. They take time and effort, and I eventually forget them." The things of the world matter most to me: having things, knowing a lot, being famous.

Good soil

"I know what's important for my eternal happiness. I make resolutions and carry them out." What matters most to me is GOD: knowing Christ, helping others and obeying my parents.

Contemplative Prayer

The most important thing for me in life should be knowing God and his will for me. That's because doing his will is the only thing that will bring me true and eternal happiness.

Contemplative prayer is the best way to get to know Jesus and to understand what he teaches me.

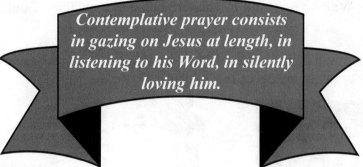

Contemplative prayer consists in gazing on Jesus at length, in listening to his Word, in silently loving him.

It can last a minute or it can last an hour. It doesn't matter how long it lasts or the time of day you pick for doing it.

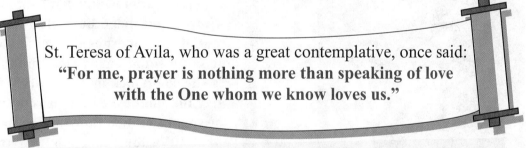

St. Teresa of Avila, who was a great contemplative, once said: **"For me, prayer is nothing more than speaking of love with the One whom we know loves us."**

What you need to do to practice contemplative prayer:

1. **Recollect your heart**. Enter into the house of God that lies within you, putting everything else aside. Dwell in his presence just as you are, not trying to hide anything from him.

2. **Gaze on God so as to get to know him**. You can't love someone you don't know. Reading his Word can help, especially a passage from the Gospels. Read the passage and place yourself in the scene, taking an active role in it. As you gaze on and study the person of Christ, try to get inside him, discovering his thoughts, his feelings, his desires, his motivations.

3. **Let him gaze on you**. His gaze will bring light to your soul and you will begin to see things as he sees them.

4. **Listen to him** with an attitude of love, obedience, and determination to carry out whatever he asks of you. Pay close attention to the thoughts God inspires in you and put them into practice in your life.

5. **Maintain silence**--internal and external. Contemplative prayer doesn't consist in long speeches or lofty thoughts, but rather brief expressions of love. Speak to Jesus from and with your heart.

Wouldn't you like to be like Jesus?

Think of two of your classmates who are very good friends. Do you see how alike they are in so many ways? From spending so much time together, from talking so much, they've come to share many of the same mannerisms and reactions to things. They often use the same words and phrases, and have the same likes and interests.

In just the same way, if you pray every day, contemplating and listening to Jesus, little by little you will start to be like him. Without realizing it, you will begin to view things and people in the same way God does.

This deep union with God will then later show itself in your love and service to others. Love can not be locked away; it must give itself away.

St. John Vianney, the "Curé of Ars," used to tell the story of a peasant who would come into his church and spend hour after hour in front of the Tabernacle, so much so that the saint would have to tell him to leave so he could lock up the church. One day the saint asked the peasant what he spent so much time talking to God about. "We don't talk about anything," the peasant replied. "I just look at him and he looks at me."

Are you ready for the battle?

If you're ready to throw yourself into the wonderful adventure of getting to know God through contemplative prayer, you're going to need to be on your guard. You're going to run into a lot of enemies who will try to stop you. These are the enemies of prayer:

First and foremost: **the devil**. He is your greatest enemy. He will do everything he can to distract you and persuade you to give up. He doesn't want you to pray and become like Jesus. He'll put ideas in your head such as "Nothing will happen if you don't pray today"; "Don't waste your time, you've got more important things to do"; "Prayer isn't the most important thing, you can always do it later."

Fill in the missing letters of your greatest enemy:

D _ _ _ L

• The second enemy of prayer is all around you: **the world**. It is made up of things which, though they may be good in themselves, can distract you and take you away from praying. Things such as your brothers and sisters, your friends, your school projects, music, television, games, etc. You need to be on your guard because it is precisely good things that the devil often uses to take you away from prayer. Don't forget: getting to know God is the most important thing in life. You need to ward off distractions so that you'll be able to spend at least a little time with him in prayer every day.

Write down the names of these good things the devil can use to take you away from prayer:

• The third enemy of prayer is part of you, it is usually referred to as "**the flesh**." Your own feelings and desires can take you away from prayer: feeling hungry or sleepy, wanting to play, etc. The devil makes use of these things, too, to stop you from praying: "You're very tired, you'd better go to bed without praying"; "You're very hungry, go eat something and then you can pray afterwards"; "You'll have a lot more fun playing, don't worry about praying."

Write down the names of these things you can feel and that can take you away from praying:

Don't forget

• The Gospel is God's own Word, the seed God wants to plant in you. God is the one who plants it. Whether or not it grows depends on you.

Soil on the edge of the path: It doesn't interest you. You just want to have a good time.
Rocky soil: You'd *like* to, but you're more worried about what others will say.
Thorny soil: You know it's the best thing, but the things of the world are more important to you.
Good soil: You realize that knowing God and his will is the most important thing, and you do everything necessary to fulfill his will.

• The best way to get to know Jesus and understand his teachings is contemplative prayer.

Knowing my faith

What is "contemplative prayer"?
Contemplative prayer consists in gazing on Jesus at length, listening to his Word, and loving him in silence.

How do I do contemplative prayer?
I must follow five steps: (1) recollect my heart; (2) gaze on God; (3) let him gaze on me; (4) listen to him; and (5) Speak little, just tell him that I love him.

What are the enemies of contemplative prayer?
The three enemies are: (1) the devil; (2) the world; and (3) the flesh.

Living my faith

• I'm going to spend some time every day in contemplative prayer so that I can get to know Jesus better and understand his teachings.

He sowed good seed

The Weeds
Chapter 3, Lesson 2

Remember
Sin is the only thing that can take you away from God.

Now you'll see
God wants you to be with him, happy forever, and it's up to you either to accept or reject his offer of friendship.

The Gospel tells us

"He proposed another parable to them. *'The kingdom of heaven may be likened to a man who sowed good seed in his field. While everyone was asleep his enemy came and sowed weeds all through the wheat, and then went off. When the crop grew and bore fruit, the weeds appeared as well. The slaves of the householder came to him and said, "Master, did you not sow good seed in your field? Where have the weeds come from?" He* answered, *"An enemy has done this." His slaves said to him, "Do you want us to go and pull them up?" He replied, "No, if you pull up the weeds you might uproot the wheat along with them. Let them grow together until harvest; then at harvest time I will say to the harvesters, 'First collect the weeds and tie them in bundles for burning; but gather the wheat into my barn.'*

"Then, dismissing the crowds, he went into the house. His disciples approached him and said, *'Explain to us the parable of the weeds in the field.'* He said in reply, *'He who sows good seed is the Son of Man, the field is the world, the good seed the children of the kingdom. The weeds are the children of the evil one, and the enemy who sows them is the devil. The harvest is the end of the age, and the harvesters are angels. Just as weeds are collected and burned up with fire, so will it be at the end of the age. The Son of Man will send his angels, and they will collect out of his kingdom all who cause others to sin and all evildoers. They will throw them into the fiery furnace, where there will be wailing and grinding of teeth. Then the righteous will shine like the sun in the kingdom of their Father. Whoever has ears ought to hear.'"*
Mt 13:24-30; 36-43

Thinking over what we have just read.

Write down here the lessons Jesus teaches us in this parable.

Connect with lines the things on the left with what they symbolize on the right.

- The sower
- The weeds
- The harvest
- The field
- The harvesters
- The seed
- The enemy
- The wheat

- The angels
- The world
- Jesus Christ
- Children of the devil
- Our good deeds
- The children of the Kingdom
- The devil
- The end of the world

Read and respond

To what are we humans called?

What should our final goal be?

What can prevent us from reaching that goal?

How do you think the devil works in the world?

What tools do you think you have for fighting against the weeds?

"Weeds" are with us in the world

**Do you remember the
story of Cain and Abel?**

"Weeds" have existed in the world ever since man freely chose to disobey God and was expelled from the earthly paradise. The devil is at work in the world and man has a natural tendency towards sin. Isn't it harder to be good than to be bad?

Find in today's newspaper three news items that show the presence of "weeds" in the world.

*1.*_____

*2.*_____

*3.*_____

Now write down three things you can do to counteract this work of the devil in the world. Talk them over with your classmates.

*1.*_____

*2.*_____

*3.*_____

Here are a few other ideas to help you fight against the weeds present in the world.

① You can't go all over the world taking care of everyone's problems. But there are four things you can do right where you are, four very effective things. Do you remember what they are? Find them in this alphabet soup:

```
l u a p o s t o l a t e d o
o r e c i p n p r a y e r a
v i g i l a n c e a e e o p
c o i c i f o r g i v e l r
```

2 The children of the evil one sowed the weeds at night when the workers were asleep. Thus the second way to fight against the weeds is to be on our guard against the weeds around us.

You are good seed. What can weeds do to your life? What are the things that can steer you away from your final goal in heaven? Write them down here:

Weed: Selfishness
What can I do to fight it?:
_____

Weed:_____
What can I do to fight it? :_____

Weed:_____
What can I do to fight it? :_____

Weed:_____
What can I do to fight it? :_____

Weed:_____
What can I do to fight it? :_____

Recall some good deeds you have done.	
Deed	Why did you do it?

If you fight against the weeds, what will the final result in your life be?

Remember that the devil invites you to do evil by putting temptations before you, but you are the one who decides to ignore them or accept them.
You must be on guard constantly so that weeds will not take root in your life.

3 A third very important way to fight weeds in your life is always to live according to God's commandments.
Find the path to heaven by connecting the dotted lines.

My goal: God

I'm going to make sure I always have more than others.

You shall not covet your neighbor's goods.

You shall not consent to impure thoughts or desires.

I'm going to see movies and look at magazines I know I shouldn't.

I'm going to take a pen that isn't mine.

You shall not lie or give false witness.

I'm going to speak badly of others.

You shall not commit impure acts.

I'm going to lie to get out of being punished.

You shall not kill.

I'm not going to take care of my body.

You shall not steal.

I'm going to be disobedient and rude.

You shall not take the name of the Lord your God in vain.

I'm not going to go to Mass next Sunday.

You shall honor your father and your mother.

My path

You shall keep holy the Sabbath.

I'm going to swear using God's name.

You shall love the Lord your God above all things.

I'm going to worry more about what I want than what God wants.

4 There are times when we give in to temptation. We sin and take a wrong turn that takes us off the road to heaven.

Jesus knew this could happen and so he instituted a sacrament that would help us get back on the right road with renewed strength. This sacrament is a sure path for reaching heaven.

Do you remember which sacrament we're talking about? Write its name here.

C _ N _ E _ _ _ I _ N

Fill in the blanks.

_____ is the sacrament that grants us _____ of the _____ committed after _____. It reconciles us with _____ and with the _____.

Church - Confession - baptism - God - forgiveness - sins

Look up verse 23 in chapter 20 of St. John's Gospel. Write down below in your own words what the verse means. After you've written your own answer, discuss the verse with your classmates.

_____
_____
_____
_____
_____
_____
_____
_____
_____
_____

There are five steps to making a good confession.

Match up the two columns:

1. Examination of conscience

○ I know I'm not perfect and because of the effects of original sin it's hard for me to avoid sinning. But I'm going to go to confession and firmly resolve not to offend God again.

2. Sorrow over one's sins

○ A way of making up for the damage caused by my sins.

3. Firm purpose of amendment

○ In God's presence, I honestly think back over the sins I have committed since my last confession.

4. Telling the priest one's sins

○ Jesus chose to give priests the power to forgive sins (Jn 20:23).

5. Carrying out the assigned penance

○ God is my Father and he wants me to be happy together with him. It makes me very sad to know that I have offended him.

What are the effects of confession? Fill in the blanks.

1. I regain the life of _____ and am reconciled with _____ and the _____.
2. I experience deep _____ and serenity in my _____.
3. I receive added strength to fight against _____.

And most important of all, confession is a sure road to my final _____, which is _____.

goal - conscience - Church - grace - God - peace - heaven - temptation

Don't forget

- God created us to be **happy forever with him.**
- God's love for us causes him to prepare us to love him back, but he doesn't force us. It is a free response that we must make all of our life. We show our love for God by keeping far from sin.
- The devil is at work in the world and in each one of us. **I am the one who chooses** to accept or reject him in my life.
- With the help of God's grace I can always overcome temptation.
- The Ten Commandments are a sure path to heaven.
- If I sin, out of God's goodness he invites me to regain and nourish my **friendship with Christ** through the **Sacrament of penance**, or confession.

Knowing my faith

What is the Sacrament of Penance, or confession?
It is the sacrament that grants us forgiveness of sins committed after baptism. It brings us back into friendship with God and the Church.

When did Christ institute the sacrament of penance?
He instituted it on Easter Sunday when he said to the apostles, "Whose ever sins you forgive, they are forgiven; whose ever sins you retain, they are retained."

What are the five steps to make a good confession?
1. Examination of conscience 2. Sorrow for one's sins 3. Firm purpose of amendment
4. Telling one's sins to the priest 5. Carrying out the penance

When is it necessary to receive the sacrament of Penance?
We must receive it whenever we have committed a serious sin, so we can be reunited to God.

Which sins must be confessed?
All mortal sins that have not been confessed before.

Living my faith

- God wants all people to be saved and be happy with him.
- I'm going to offer up a sacrifice every day for those people I don't know but who are far away from God. I'm going to ask God to help them find their way to him.
- I'm also going to go to confession since it will help me fight against weeds and be even closer to God.

Power in the Little Things

The Leaven and Dough
Chapter 3, Lesson 3

Remember
God has called you to help him save the world.
Now you'll see
God loves to use the smallest things to accomplish the greatest and most important things.

The Gospel tells us

"He proposed another parable to them. *'The kingdom of heaven is like a mustard seed that a person took and sowed in a field. It is the smallest of all the seeds, yet when full-grown it is the largest of plants. It becomes a large bush, and the birds of the sky come and dwell in its branches.'* He spoke to them another parable. *'The kingdom of heaven is like yeast that a woman took and mixed with three measures of wheat flour until the whole batch was leavened'.*"

Mt 13: 31-33

Study these drawings.

The seed that begins to sprout is

The Gospel

The bit of leaven is

_____.
(write your name)

The sower is

The apostle _____
(write your name)

The women who kneads the leaven into the dough is

God places you in the world.

The tree is

The Church, which embraces all people.

The dough that rises thanks to the leaven is

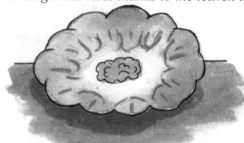

The world, which is transformed thanks to the example you give.

Think about the above drawings in silence and then discuss your thoughts with your classmates.

Remember

When you were baptized you became a child of God and a member of the Church, whose head is Christ himself. As a member of the Church, you share in Christ's functions as Priest, Prophet, and King.

Priest The priest is the one who "offers sacrifices," who renders things "sacred."

You carry out your priestly functions by rendering all you do "sacred." When you convert all that you do into acts of praise for God; all that you do at home with your family, your work and study time, your games and sports, your time with your friends, and your prayers you make these things holy. All of this is pleasing to God if you carry it out with joy, patience, and love and if you offer it all up to him, uniting it to the gifts offered up to him at Mass during the offertory.

Prophet This means being a "witness"

You carry out your prophetic functions when you let others know about Christ through your words and example.

King This means "one who governs"

You fulfill your kingly functions when you govern, or master, yourself; not letting yourself be governed by your passions, temptations, or by what others say.

You also carry out your kingly functions when you succeed in transforming the world around you, as Christ intended.

Don't forget to govern also means to serve others. Thus a good king will always think of others and try to find ways to resolve problems so that all his subjects will be happier.

Engaging in apostolate is a duty for every Catholic Christian. It is the duty to help God expand his Kingdom.

We can engage in real apostolate through our words and our actions, bringing others to know and love Christ; we can also do apostolate through our example, transforming the world from within.

To be an apostle means being a soldier of Christ.
The Gospel is your key to victory.
Your strength will come from prayer.

The state of the world today

- A lot of people don't know Christ, and not just those in far-away countries. People very close to you don't know him: friends, workers, neighbors, etc.
- Things are turned upside down: Instead of God governing man, and man the world, the world now governs man and man ignores God.
- The devil uses music, TV, advertising, and much more, to promote ideas and life styles contrary to the will of God.

If you were king of the whole world

What would you do to make the world a better place?

Activity

With the help of your mother or father, cut out of the newspaper or a magazine a news item or advertisement that shows very clearly that people need to hear the message of the Gospel. Paste it in the box. Below, write down what is wrong and how it can be corrected.

Through baptism God gave you kingly functions. List some things you see in the world that are not in agreement with Christ's teachings.

What do you think you could do to change these things?

What can you do to help others?

Draw a circle around the things that you think will help in preaching the Gospel to others:

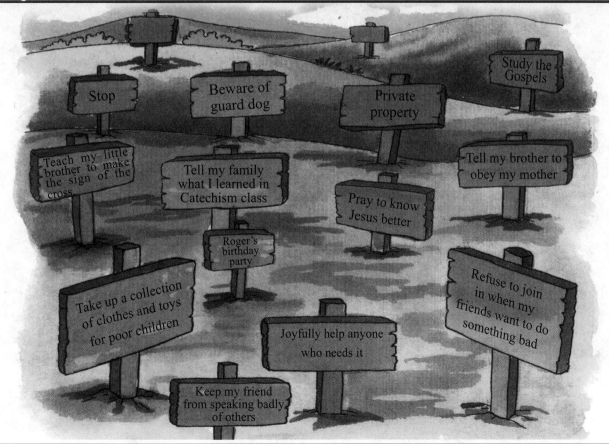

Don't forget

- The Gospel is the seed that grows in the world. You need to help sow it in hearts everywhere.
- You are the leaven God has placed in the world to transform it from within.
- Through your baptism you share in Christ's functions as Priest, Prophet, and King.

Knowing my faith

How can you carry out your functions as priest?
By offering all that I do to God, thus sanctifying it.

How can you carry out your functions as prophet?
By preaching the Gospel through my words and actions.

How can you carry out your functions as king?
By making sure that everything I do is in line with God's will, and by doing all I can to make everything around me conform to his will.

What is "apostolate"?
Engaging in apostolate is the duty of every Christian, the duty of helping God expand his Kingdom.

How can we engage in apostolate?
Apostolate can be done in two ways:
1. Through our words and actions, bringing others to know and love Christ
2. Through our example, transforming the world from within

Living my faith

- I'm going to reflect on the things that happen around me, seeing which ones are not in agreement with the Gospel. Then I'm going to take real steps to turn them around.

Look What I Found!

The Treasure and the Pearl
Chapter 3, Lesson 4

Remember
at baptism you received God's grace.
Now you're going to see
God's grace is a priceless treasure since it keeps you united to your best friend, Jesus.

The Gospel tells us
"'The kingdom of heaven is like a treasure buried in a field, which a person finds and hides again, and out of joy goes and sells all that he has and buys that field. Again, the kingdom of heaven is like a merchant searching for fine pearls. When he finds a pearl of great price, he goes and sells all that he has and buys it.'"

Mt 13:44-46

Reflect on what you think Jesus wants to teach you through this parable.

Write it down here and talk it over with your classmates.
Now answer these questions: What did the men in the parables find?
Why did they sell everything they had?
What were their reactions when they came across the treasure and the pearl?

Here you have some pearls.
Number them according to the value each one has for you.

A video game

An afternoon at the mall

Designer clothes

Getting good grades

Vacation with my family

My friendship with Jesus

My friend _____

A group project well executed

Being able to help a friend

Write down here the two pearls of greatest value for you and what you are going to do to acquire them.

The pearls I want most	What I am going to do

Study the photos and then fill in the blanks.

baptism - grace - friend - Jesus

At my _____ *I*
received the life of _____
and _____ *became my*
best _____.

Do you remember the commitments you entered into with God on the day of your baptism?

Write them down here:

_____
_____
_____

You no doubt got a lot of presents on the day of your Baptism, but that was a long time ago and you were too small to remember. Who knows where those presents are now! You also received another gift that day, the greatest gift ever, one that is ever-fresh and which you should never lose.

There are two kinds of grace:

Habitual, or sanctifying grace:
This is a habitual gift which gives us a share in the divine life of the Trinity.

Grace means having God within you.

Actual grace:
This is a special grace from God at a specific moment in time. It helps us grow in holiness and be closer to God.

A friend is a true treasure. Don't you agree?

My best friends are:

_____
_____
_____

Some things that build friendships:

_____
_____
_____

Somethings that destroy friendships:

_____
_____
_____

Ways to mend a broken friendship:

_____
_____
_____

Am I a good friend to Jesus?

Jesus is my very best friend.

Check off the things you need to do to be a good friend:

- help my friends to be better people_____
- treat my friends with disrespect_____
- rejoice when things go well for them_____
- be with them when things are going bad for them_____
- invite them to see or listen to things beyond my age_____
- get them to go to Communion_____
- accept my friends as they are_____

Write three things that will build your friendship with Jesus.	Write three things that can weaken or destroy your friendship with Jesus.

Do you remember the only thing that can break off your friendship with Jesus? _____
What sacrament enables you to regain the life of grace? _____

I don't want to go to Confession!

What would you say to a friend who doesn't want to go to Confession and gives you the following reasons. Discuss them with your classmates, and then match them up with the responses below.

I don't feel like it. I'll go next week. ◯

I'm ashamed. What's Fr. X going to say? ◯

I'm pretty sure all my sins are venial ones. ◯

Fr. X is very strict. He'll really bawl me out. ◯

I don't know what I'll say. ◯

I always confess the same sins and never get any better. ◯

I prefer to confess my sins directly to God. ◯

1. You won't have this problem if you make a good examination of conscience. Look back over your day every night to see where you've slipped up. This will make it easier for you to prepare your confession.

2. This is natural. The same things trouble us all: we're lazy, selfish, and proud. What you need to do is sincerely resolve to do better, and take the necessary steps to get there. Besides, the point of confession is not to say different sins every time.

3. Fr. X isn't going to say anything. He's there to give you God's forgiveness.

4. Don't lose the chance to be in the state of grace. If you wait a week, you'll lose a week of being close to your best friend. Anyway, don't forget that we always need to be ready for anything.

5. Even though your sins may be only venial ones and you don't *have* to go to confession, this sacrament will give you added strength to overcome future temptations and to avoid falling into mortal sin.

6. Jesus gave the power to forgive sins to the apostles and to priests. If you go to confession you can be absolutely certain that your sins are forgiven the moment the priest gives you absolution.

7. Remember that the priest is only human, too, and might be tired or overworked. The important thing is getting God's forgiveness, even if it means the priest speaks a bit harshly to us.

Don't forget

- The **life of grace** is a priceless treasure and we need to work to preserve it.
- **Friendship with Christ** is the most valuable pearl we could ever possess.
- The life of **grace** is the presence of God in our souls, which we first received on the day of our baptism.
- Through the sacrament of **Reconciliation** we regain and/or strengthen our friendship with Christ.

Knowing my faith

What is "grace"?
It is the presence of God in one's soul.

How many kinds of grace are there?
There are two kinds: habitual, or sanctifying grace, and actual grace.

What is habitual or sanctifying grace?
It is the presence of God in the soul. Thanks to it we can live in God and do everything out of love for him.

What is actual grace?
This is a special grace from God at a specific moment in time. It helps us grow in holiness and be closer to God.

Living my faith

- From now on, my friendship with Christ is going to be the most important thing in my life. I'm going to go to the chapel to visit Jesus and ask him never to let me be separated from him.

- I'm going to encourage a friend to go to confession and to get into the habit of going regularly. I'm going to prepare my own confessions very well, full of determination not to offend God anymore and to take steps actually possible to become a true witness of Jesus for those around me.

The Parables of the Kingdom
Chapter 3
Review

Match up the two columns.

1. Consists in gazing on Jesus, listening to him, and silently loving him.

2. The sower and the seed represent.

3. The three enemies of prayer are.

4. Keeping these is a sure road to heaven.

5. The weeds and wheat represent.

6. There are these many steps to making a good confession.

7. The Kingdom of God is like a.

8. The presence of God in the soul.

9. Actual grace is.

10. Through baptism, we share in Christ's.

11. The two ways for engaging in apostolate are.

12. Prayer is the food that nourishes.

- the Ten Commandments
- Contemplative prayer
- the devil, the world, and the flesh
- God and his Word
- those who are good and those who are evil in the world
- apostolic action
- functions as Priest, Prophet, and King
- five
- by example
- by word and action
- a special help from God at a specific moment in time
- treasure hidden in a field

Study the following words:

Parable; Wealth; Contemplative; Leaven; Priest; Weeds; Confession

Fill in the missing letters:

P __ r __ b __ e; W __ __ l __ __ __; C __ nt __ __pl __ t __ v __; __ ea __ e __;

W __ __ __ s; C __ __ f __ __ __ __ __ __ n.

Jesus, the Performer of Miracles

Chapter 4

The Wind and the Sea Obey Him!

The calming of the storm
Chapter 4, Lesson 1

Remember
Jesus has full power over the forces of nature.

Now you'll see
God has invited you to help him in the work of Creation.

The Gospel tells us

"He got into a boat and his disciples followed him. Suddenly a violent storm came up on the sea, so that the boat was being swamped by waves; but he was asleep. They came and woke him, saying, *'Lord, save us! We are perishing!'* He said to them, *'Why are you terrified, O you of little faith?'* Then he got up, rebuked the winds and the sea, and there was great calm. The men were amazed and said, *'What sort of man is this, whom even the winds and the sea obey?'"*

Mt 8:23-27

Think over the following questions and then raise your hand to share your answers with the rest of the class. Write down the correct answers afterwards.

Why was Jesus able to calm the storm? Why did the wind and sea obey him?

_____

_____

Do you know anyone else whom the wind and sea obey?

_____

_____

_____

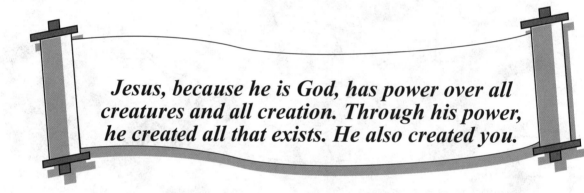

Jesus, because he is God, has power over all creatures and all creation. Through his power, he created all that exists. He also created you.

Do you remember what the following titles mean?

Match up the columns by connecting them with lines.

- God
- God is all-powerful
- God is Creator
- Jesus is the Son of God
- Jesus is Lord

- Jesus is God himself made man
- God created from nothing everything that exists
- The beginning and end of all things
- Jesus is Lord over all that exists
- Nothing is impossible for him

Carefully study the photographs and choose the words that you think best describe them.

- *Horrible*

- *Beautiful*

- *Ugly*

- *Good*

- *Perfect*

- *Uninteresting*

- *Bad*

- *Disorderly*

- *Harmonious*

God created all things

Throughout history people have always asked the same questions when they contemplated the wonders of nature. *"How did the universe come to be?"* *"Who or what created it all?"* *"Who created man?"*

From the Bible we know that God is the Creator of everything that exists. If you want to go over the Creation account again, you can read it in the Book of Genesis, Chapter 1, verses 1 - 27.

The things God created are good

After recounting the creation of the different things in nature, the Book of Genesis says: "...and God saw that it was good."

It was out of love that God created all the beauty and richness of the world. The **Love of God** is the source of everything we see around us: the universe, plants, animals, and humans, even the things we can not see. The things created by God have something in common: they are good, perfect, and beautiful. **God's goodness** is reflected in all that he does. If you study the order and harmony of the universe, in living things and even the smallest things you can see, you'll see the **Wisdom of God** reflected. Contemplating the things God has created enables us to get an idea of his **greatness**.

God created man

In the Biblical account, man stands out as the most important part of creation. God makes man in his own image and likeness, endowing him with **intelligence, will, and freedom**. This renders man capable of **knowing** God, communicating with him, and **loving** him. It also makes him capable of loving his **fellowman**.

God created the world for man

God creates man to be the lord of creation, handing creation over to man so that he can
• learn the secrets of nature, discovering and mastering its laws
• master nature and use it for good
• transform and perfect the world
• help God to continue the work of creation

How does man participate in the work of Creation?

By cultivating the land   extracting minerals   manufacturing products   building houses

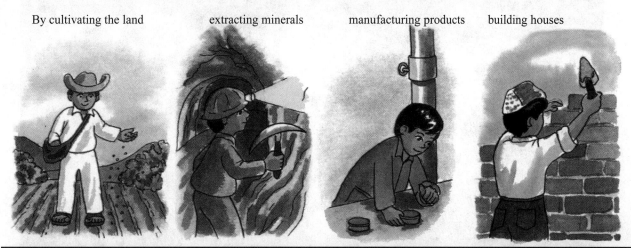

Write down three other things man does to further the work of Creation:

_____

_____

_____

How can you participate in the work of Creation?

Write underneath each drawing what these children are doing to help carry on the work of Creation:

_____

_____

_____

_____

_____

Three prayers. Three men. One Creator.

A Psalm of King David

When I see your heavens,
the work of your fingers
the moon and the stars which you set in place -
What are humans that you are mindful of them,
mere mortals that you care for them?
Yet you have made them little less than a god,
crowned them with glory and honor.
You have given them rule over the works of
your hands,
putting all things at their feet:
All sheep and oxen,
even the beasts of the field.
The birds of the air, the fishes of the sea,
and whatever swims the paths of the seas.
O Lord, our Lord, how awesome is your name
through all the earth!
(Psalm 8)

A Song for All God's Creatures

May you be blessed, O God, for all that you
have created,
and especially blessed for brother Sun
who lights up and opens the day
and is beautiful in his splendor,
proclaiming in the heavens news of his
Author.
And for sister water, precious in her clarity,
useful, chaste and humble,
for her may you be blessed O God!
And for sister earth who is blessing upon
blessing,
our mother and our sister, who gives in every
season
herbs, fruits and flowers of every color,
who sustains and rules us:
for her may you be blessed O God!
And for those who, out of love for you,
forgive and put up with bodily evils and
tribulation.
Blessed are those who serenely endure pain
for consolation will come to them.
And for brother death: May you be blessed O
God!
No living thing escapes your visitation.
Blessed are those who do the will of God!
Serve him with tenderness and humility of
heart,
be grateful for his gifts, praise his Creation!
Every created thing--bless the Lord!
Amen.
St. Francis of Assisi

Creation Song

I love the wonders of the world I see
because You have given me eyes to see them.
I love the songs of the universe
because You have given me ears to hear
them.
I love the intoxicating fragrance of your
flowers
because You have given me the sense of
smell
to enjoy them.
I love the fruit of your trees
because You have given me the sense of taste
to savor them.
I love you, Lord, in the beauty of your things
for one of your names is the Beautiful One.
Wherever I go, it is you, Lord, that I see.
And since all things exist for you,
I feel you in all things.
They are your sons and daughters.
I, too, am a son of yours.
Thus I am a brother of all things
and want to love all things,
from the smallest brother-pebble
to the brightest sister-flower...
They are your multi-colored message,
a living, breathing reminder of you.
They tell me that you are still there,
watching over the least of your creations...

Study the three psalms/songs and respond.

What do the three have in common? Put a "T" in the circle if the statement is True and an "F" if it is False.

Each prayer praises God. ◯

They all show love for nature. ◯

They reveal respect for created things. ◯

They express gratitude to God for creation. ◯

Make up your own Creation Song.

Creation Song

Remember

- Jesus, because he is God, has complete power over all created things.
- We can't see God, but by studying the things he has created we can form some notion of his Love, Wisdom, Goodness, and Power.

Knowing my faith

Who is the beginning and end of all things?
God is the beginning and end of all things.

What does it mean that God is the "Creator"?
It means that he created from nothing everything that exists.

Why did God hand Creation over to man?
So that man would study it, master it, and use it for good.

How does man share in God's work of Creation?
Man shares in the task of Creation through the work he does.

Living my faith

- I'm going to look more carefully at the things created by God, trying to see him in them and thus know him better and love him more.
- I'm going to make the most of everything God has given me for helping him in the work of creation.
- I'm going to take care of my body and develop my mind by studying hard. That way I'll be of greater use to all of creation and will be able to help others when they need it.

Jesus, Save Me!

Jesus Walks on Water
Chapter 4, Lesson 2

Remember
Mary teaches you to always trust in God.

Now you will see
you can always trust in Jesus and that he has many ways of helping you.

The Gospel tells us

"Then he made the disciples get into the boat and precede him to the other side, while he dismissed the crowds. After doing so, he went up on the mountain by himself to pray. When it was evening he was there alone. Meanwhile the boat, already a few miles offshore, was being tossed about by the waves, for the wind was against it. During the fourth watch of the night, he came toward them, walking on the sea. When the disciples saw him walking on the sea they were terrified. *'It is a ghost,'* they said, and they cried out in fear. At once Jesus spoke to them, *'Take courage, it is I; do not be afraid.'* Peter said to him in reply, *'Lord, if it is you, command me to come to you on the water.'* He said, *'Come.'* Peter got out of the boat and began to walk on the water toward Jesus. But when he saw how strong the wind was he became frightened; and, beginning to sink, he cried out, *'Lord, save me!'* Immediately Jesus stretched out his hand and caught him, and said to him, *'O you of little faith, why did you doubt?'* After they got into the boat, the wind died down. Those who were in the boat did him homage, saying, *'Truly, you are the Son of God.'*"

Mt 14:22-33

Put the drawings in their proper order by writing numbers in the circles.

The storm and heavy waves took the disciples' boat far out into the sea. You will have to face storms and heavy waves in your life, too, hard times that could make you drift away from God.

What are some of the storms in your life?

Write here some hard things someone your age might have to face.

Difficult situations	Who can help you?

We trust in them

There are some things we can't do all on our own. We need the help of others. When we are faced with problems, we turn to those who can help us: either our parents, teachers, friends, or a priest.

Under each photo write what you see and discuss with your classmates.

This boy can't move the pew on his own. Who is helping him?

_____

How is this mother helping her child? _____

These students don't understand the day's lesson. What is the teacher doing to help them understand?

_____

How can the priest help these children?

_____

Friends, parents, teachers, and priests can all help us. They know how to help us and we turn to them often. Yet there is someone else who can **always** help you, one you can always trust and turn to. Who is it? _____

Save me, Lord!

Peter cried out to Jesus for help when he began to sink. He knew that Jesus could help him. Like Peter, you should trust in Jesus and ask him to help you, especially when things get tough. To do this, you need to practice one of the three **theological virtues**. Find it here:

n	o	p	l	e	s	t	e	r
a	n	b	a	u	n	o	o	m
i	t	d	h	o	p	e	s	h
o	u	e	f	t	p	l	g	e
h	o	m	t	s	c	o	j	g

Do you remember me?

I lived long before Christ was born. I am the father of God's chosen people, Israel. God made a promise to me and I always trusted in him. I always lived full of hope because I knew that God always keeps his promises.

To test me, God ordered me to offer my son as a sacrifice. I know if I trusted God nothing bad would happen. He always helped me and my family in everything.

Who am I? _____

St. Paul speaks to us about hope.

Look up St. Paul's letter to the Romans in the New Testament. Find chapter 12, verse 12, and write it down here:

"
_____
_____."

What do you think this verse means?

_____
_____

The virtue of hope gives us the confidence that we will get to heaven, because that's what Christ has promised us if we are faithful to his teachings.
Through hope, we put our trust in Jesus and in his ability to help us in our difficulties, just as he helped Peter.

God wants us to ask him for what we need, full of hope, in the same way that Peter cried out, **"Save me, Lord!"**

In prayers of petition we turn to God, our Father, the one who created us, and ask him to help us. God loves us and listens to us in our needs. He is aware of our needs and longs to help us.

Look up the following passages in the New Testament. Write down the thoughts each passage inspires in you and discuss them with your friends.

The Letter of James, chapter 1, verses 5 & 6.

The letter to the Philippians, chapter 4, verse 6.

_____
_____
_____
_____

_____
_____
_____
_____

St. Matthew, chapter 7, verses 7 & 8.

_____
_____
_____
_____

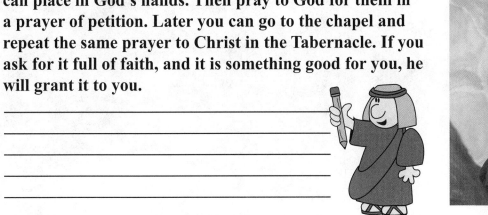

Don't forget that you can ask Jesus for anything you need! Write down the needs you have right now and which you can place in God's hands. Then pray to God for them in a prayer of petition. Later you can go to the chapel and repeat the same prayer to Christ in the Tabernacle. If you ask for it full of faith, and it is something good for you, he will grant it to you.

_____
_____
_____
_____
_____
_____
_____

Don't forget

- Just as he did with Peter, **Jesus can save you** during difficult moments in life.
- You should have full **confidence** in Jesus since he is always able to help you.
- You are all weak and need **God.**
- The virtue of **hope** brings us to hope and trust in God and his promises.
- Always ask **God** for everything you need, and do so full of trust in him.

Knowing my faith

What is the virtue of hope?
It is the theological virtue by which we desire the kingdom of heaven and eternal life as our happiness, placing our trust in God's promises and the help of his grace.

Living my faith

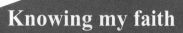

- I know that **God always wants to help me in my needs.** I'm going to go to the chapel to ask Jesus to help me in my needs, and to tell him that I trust in him. I'm going to get a friend to go with me.
- As I live each day, especially when things become difficult, I'm going to tell God over and over that **I need his help and that I trust in him.**
- I'm going to remember that there are **a lot of people around me that need help.** I'm going to see how I can help them.

He Picked up his Mat and Left

A Paralytic is Cured
Chapter 4, Lesson 3

Remember.
Jesus had the power to cure the sick and the lame.

Now you're going to see
God hates sin but loves sinners.

The Gospel tells us

"When Jesus returned to Capernaum after some days, it became known that he was at home. Many gathered together so that there was no longer room for them, not even around the door, and he preached the word to them. They came bringing to him a paralytic carried by four men. Unable to get near Jesus because of the crowd, they opened up the roof above him. After they had broken through, they let down the mat on which the paralytic was lying. When Jesus saw their faith, he said to the paralytic, *'Child, your sins are forgiven.'* Now some of the scribes were sitting there asking themselves, *'Why does this man speak that way? He is blaspheming. Who but God alone can forgive sins?'* Jesus immediately knew in his mind what they were thinking to themselves, so he said, *'Why are you thinking such things in your hearts? Which is easier, to say to the paralytic, "Your sins are forgiven," or to say, "Rise, pick up your mat and walk"? But that you may know that the Son of Man has authority to forgive sins on earth'*- he said to the paralytic, *'I say to you, rise, pick up your mat, and go home.'* He rose, picked up his mat at once, and went away in the sight of everyone. They were all astounded and glorified God, saying, *'We have never seen anything like this.'*"

Mk 2:1-12

Activity

Look up the following words in the dictionary and then write in your own words what they mean:

Paralytic:_____

Blasphemy:_____

Look over the Gospel passage again and answer the following questions:

What was the first thing Jesus said to the paralytic?

'Child, your _____ are _____.'

Why did the scribes think Jesus was committing blasphemy?

_____

_____

What did Jesus do to show them that he had the power to forgive sins?

_____

_____

Remember how Jesus calmed the storm?
How he walked on water?
How he multiplied the loaves and fishes?

*Jesus showed us **his power over created things** in many ways.*

When he cured the paralytic and forgave his sins, Jesus showed us his power over sickness and over sin.

What is sin?

Picture this: You invited a friend to sleep over and he said he would come. You get everything ready to have a great time together. Your mother fixes your friend's favorite meal. You get out all your best games and toys. You rent a video to watch after dinner. Suddenly your friend calls and says.

Guess what? I'm not going to be coming over. Billy's invited me over to his house and so I'm going to sleep over at his house instead.

How would this make you feel?

Underline the words that best describe how you would feel:

- SAD
- HAPPY
- HURT
- GRATEFUL
- OFFENDED
- REJECTED
- JOYFUL

God has invited you to the most wonderful place you could ever imagine, where you can be happy with him forever. He created you and gave you everything you have. He sent his Son to earth so that you would be able to go to heaven. He shows you the way there through the Commandments, your conscience, and messengers he places all around you. The only thing he wants is for you to be happy forever. When you do something wrong, when you sin, it's as if you said to him:

"No thanks, God. I'm not interested in your heaven. I don't want to be your friend. I'm more interested in the things the world and the devil have to offer me. Thanks anyway."

How do you think that makes God feel? Think it over in silence and then share your thoughts with the rest of your class.

To sin is to offend God's love for us.

When do we commit sin?

We sin when we do evil, when we disobey God and rebel against the things he has taught us. When he sins, man tries to make himself God. He thinks he knows everything and can do everything on his own. He tries to fabricate his own kind of "good," ignoring any guidance from God, who loves man and seeks what is truly good for him.

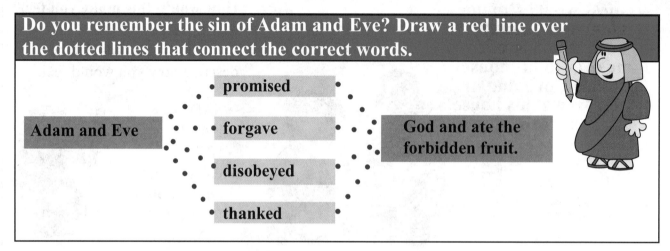

Do you remember the sin of Adam and Eve? Draw a red line over the dotted lines that connect the correct words.

Adam and Eve

promised
forgave
disobeyed
thanked

God and ate the forbidden fruit.

Are all sins equally serious?

There are mortal and venial sins.
Mortal sins completely destroy love, killing the life of grace and the presence of God in our souls. They separate us from God, rupturing our friendship with him.

For a sin to be mortal the three following conditions must be present:
1. *Grave matter:* The act committed must be truly evil, a clear breaking of one of the Ten Commandments.
2. *Full knowledge:* This means knowing perfectly well that the act to be committed is sinful, an offense against God and the Church.
3. *Full consent:* The act is committed freely, without any outside pressure. One chooses freely to perform the act.

Mortal sin shuts us out of the kingdom of heaven and condemns us to eternal death in hell.

Venial sins wound and weaken love but do not destroy it.
Although it doesn't break off our friendship with God, venial sin greatly weakens that friendship. Venial sin prevents you from growing in holiness. This is why it is so *very dangerous*, it darkens one's conscience little by little. Repeated venial sins turn into "vices" which are very hard to break and which halt spiritual progress.

Are there certain sins that give birth to others?

Yes. Certain sins are the root-cause of many other sins and are called **CAPITAL SINS.** They are:

Pride: thinking you're the best, you don't need God or anyone else, other people are nothing compared to you.

Greed: wanting more and more things, just to have them; refusing to share them with anyone.

Lust: degrading the idea of love through selfish desires.

Envy: becoming bitter and angry when someone does better than you or has more than you.

Anger: losing your temper to the point of verbally or physically hurting others.

Gluttony: Letting yourself be taken over by an immoderate longing for food or drink, even to the point of doing ourselves harm.

Laziness: always wanting the easiest way out and neglecting your duties; unwilling to do anything that requires real effort.

Can we fall into sin by participating in the sins of others?

Yes. We also sin when we collaborate in the sins of others:
• Helping to plan out a sinful act, even if we don't carry it out ourselves.
• Praising or approving the sin of another.
• Advising another to do something sinful.
• Neglecting to prevent another from sinning when we can.
• Hiding or protecting someone who has sinned.
• Directly or indirectly helping another to commit a sin.

Where do sins come from?

Sins come from within us. The human heart is the source of every sin we see around us.

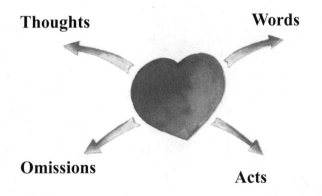

Thoughts

Words

Omissions

Acts

The root to sin in the world lies in the human heart.

The heart is also the source of all good deeds.

Cross out the evil acts that come from the girl's heart, and draw a circle around the good acts.

God hates the sin but loves the sinner

Look up the passage of the repentant sinner in Luke 7:36.

Draw a picture about Jesus forgiving the sinful woman.

"Your many sins are forgiven you, for you have loved greatly. He who loves little is forgiven little."

Only God can forgive sins

Jesus Christ, because he is God, has the power to forgive sins.
Christ gives priests the power to forgive sins in his name.

When Jesus appeared to his disciples for the first time after the Resurrection, he said to them:

"Receive the Holy Spirit. Whose ever sins you forgive, they are forgiven them. Whose ever sins you retain, they are retained." **(Jn 20: 22-23).**

God hasn't set up any direct lines to heaven

Instead, he set up his Church to be the instrument of forgiveness for sinners. He could have set things up differently, but this is the way he chose to do it.

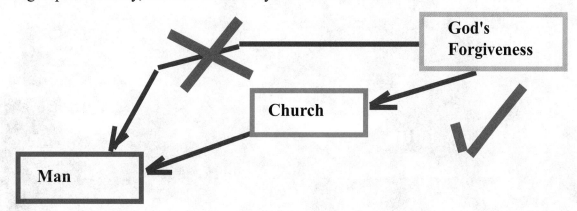

This is why it doesn't work to say, "I confess my sins to God directly." He is the one who chose to forgive us through his priests.

Christ himself is the one who acts through the priest

Christ instituted a sacrament to give another chance to anyone who falls into mortal sin after baptism.

Do you remember the name of this sacrament? Fill in the missing letters:

R _ _ _ _ _ _ _ _ _ _ _ _ _ _ N

The following words are the formula the priest uses in confession to forgive us our sins. Read it over carefully and then answer the questions.

"God, the Father of mercies, through the death and resurrection of his Son has reconciled the world to himself and sent the Holy Spirit among us for the forgiveness of sins. Through the ministry of the Church *may God give you pardon and peace*, and *I absolve you from your sins in the name of the Father, and of the Son, and of the Holy Spirit."*

Who is the one who gives pardon and peace?

_____

Who absolves you from your sins?

_____

In whose name does he absolve them?

_____

Don't forget

- Jesus showed us his power over creation in many different ways.
- When Jesus cured the paralytic he showed his power over sickness and sin.
- Jesus gave the apostles the power to forgive sins when he said to them, "Receive the Holy Spirit. Whose ever sins you forgive, they are forgiven them. Whose ever sins you retain, they are retained." (Jn 20:23)

Knowing my faith

1. Where does the root of all sin in the world lie?
In the human heart.

2. What is sin?
Sin is an offense against God's love for us.

3. How are sins divided, based on their seriousness?
They can be divided into mortal and venial sins.

4. What are the three conditions for a sin to be mortal?
1. Grave matter 2. Full knowledge 3. Full consent

5. What happens if a person dies in mortal sin?
He or she cannot go to heaven and is condemned to eternal death in hell.

6. Who can forgive sins?
Any Catholic priest who has received this power from Christ and the Church.

7. Who gave the apostles the power to forgive sins?
Christ did when he said to them, "Receive the Holy Spirit. Whose ever sins you forgive, they are forgiven them. Whose ever sins you retain, they are retained."

8. Who is it that forgives sin?
Jesus Christ forgives sin, through his priests.

Living my faith

This week I'm going to encourage my friends, siblings, and parents to go to Confession, full of trust in God.

Look at all this Bread!

The Multiplication of the Loaves and Fishes
Chapter 4, Lesson 4

Remember
Jesus longs to help you.

Now you'll see
Jesus can give you everything you need since he has the power to do so.

The Gospel tells us
"When Jesus heard of it, he withdrew in a boat to a deserted place by himself. The crowds heard of this and followed him on foot from their towns. When he disembarked and saw the vast crowd, his heart was moved with pity for them, and he cured their sick. When it was evening, the disciples approached him and said, *'This is a deserted place and it is already late; dismiss the crowds so that they can go to the villages and buy food for themselves.'* Jesus said to them, *'There is no need for them to go away; give them some food yourselves.'* But they said to him, *'Five loaves and two fish are all we have here.'* Then he said, *'Bring them here to me,'* and he ordered the crowds to sit down on the grass. Taking the five loaves and the two fish, and looking up to heaven, he said the blessing, broke the loaves, and gave them to the disciples, who in turn gave them to the crowds. They all ate and were satisfied, and they picked up the fragments left over--twelve wicker baskets full. Those who ate were about five thousand men, not counting women and children." **Mt 14:13-21**

Answer the following questions:

Why were the people following Jesus? _____

What did Jesus do for them? _____

What did the disciples say? _____

What did Jesus say to them in reply? _____

What lesson does Jesus teach us in this passage? _____

Why was Jesus able to help the people? _____

How can you apply it to your own life? _____

Write down what each phrase means:

"He felt pity for them" _____

"They don't need to go away" _____

"You give them something to eat" _____

Jesus is concerned with all our needs, both physical and spiritual

We can follow Christ's example by helping our neighbor. The "Works of Mercy" are a way of living out Christ's teachings. These "works" are:

Spiritual: Helping our neighbor in his or her spiritual needs
Corporal: Helping our neighbor in his or her physical needs

Fill in the blanks below, and then connect each phrase to the correct word on the right.

patiently - homeless - sorrowful - visit - offenses - correct
- living - hungry - clothe - teach - bury

Corporal

- Feed the _____.
- Give shelter to the _____.
- _____ the ignorant.
- _____ the naked.
- Console the _____.
- _____ the sick and imprisoned.
- Forgive _____.
- _____ those who are in error.
- _____ bear the mistakes of others.
- Pray to God for the _____ and the dead.

Spiritual

Think back over the past week. In what ways did you lend a hand to your neighbor? Write them down here.

_____

_____

_____

St. Rose of Lima's mother was upset once with her for bringing sick and homeless people into their home. St. Rose replied, "When we serve the poor and the sick, we serve Jesus. We should never tire of serving our neighbor, because through them we serve Jesus."

The world we live in

Next to each photo write what you see in it and which work of mercy you could perform to help out.

This boy has many toys, but he doesn't have any brothers and sisters or friends to play with.	These children live in the streets and only eat when someone gives them a handout. Even so, they know Jesus and are happy with the little they have.

Try to imagine the needs of the boy on the left and the children on the right.

What are the needs of the boy on the left?
Corporal: _____
Spiritual: _____
How could you help him? _____

What are the needs of the children on the right?
Corporal: _____
Spiritual: _____
How could you help them? _____

Let's plan a group project!

Plan a project to help others in their needs, just as Jesus has taught us to do.

Ask your parents to help you. They no doubt are aware of some place that has lots of needs, a soup kitchen, homeless shelter, orphanage, etc. Get the address and telephone number. Find out what their most pressing needs are and then get together with your friends to draw up a plan of action. What will you be able to accomplish in the next twelve months?

Institution: _____

Address: _____

Telephone: _____

Contact person: _____

Urgent needs: _____

Project Calendar

In: _____ (month) We will: _____

In: _____ We will: _____

In: _____ We will: _____

In: _____ We will: _____

In: _____ We will: _____

In: _____ We will: _____

In: _____ We will: _____

In: _____ We will: _____

In: _____ We will: _____

In: _____ We will: _____

In: _____ We will: _____

In: _____ We will: _____

"I assure you that whatever you do for the least of my brothers you do for me." (Mt 25:40)

"I was hungry and you fed me, I was thirsty and you gave me to drink, I was a stranger and you welcomed me, I was naked and you clothed me, I was sick and you visited me, imprisoned, and you came to see me." (Mt 25:35-36)

By miraculously multiplying the loaves and fishes, Jesus took care of the physical needs of the people who followed him. But he was also concerned with their spiritual needs. Can you recall an episode from Christ's life when he showed his concern for people's spiritual needs?

_____

_____

Write down what this phrase from the Gospel means: "I am the bread of life. Whoever eats this bread will live forever."

_____

_____

*What Sacrament is Christ talking about?*_____

In the **Sacrament of the Eucharist** Christ takes care of our **spiritual** needs.

Just as your body needs nourishment to grow healthy and strong, so your soul also needs the spiritual nourishment Christ gives us in the Eucharist.

Match up the columns and you'll see what the Eucharist does for you:

1. The Eucharist deepens our friendship and union with Christ because...

2. The Eucharist frees us from venial sin because...

3. The Eucharist keeps us from committing mortal sin because...

4. The Eucharist builds up the unity of the Mystical Body of Christ, that is, the Church, because...

5. The Eucharist moves us to help those in need because...

◯ it builds up charity within us, and venial sins are wiped out by living out this charity.

◯ those who receive Christ in the Eucharist become more closely united to Christ, who draws us into one single body.

◯ it preserves, deepens, and renews the life of grace and friendship with Christ we received at baptism.

◯ as we become a better and better friend of Christ's it will be harder for us to rupture this friendship by committing a serious sin.

◯ it makes us see Christ in the needy.

Don't forget

- Christ takes care of all our needs, both **spiritual and physical.**
- By performing the **Works of Mercy** we follow the example of Christ.
- In the **Eucharist** Christ becomes bread to satisfy all our spiritual needs.

Knowing my faith

The Corporal Works of Mercy are:
- feeding the hungry
- giving drink to the thirsty
- sheltering the homeless
- clothing the naked
- visiting the sick and imprisoned
- burying the dead

The Spiritual Works of Mercy are:
- teaching the ignorant
- charitably correcting those in error
- consoling the sorrowful
- forgiving those who offend us
- patiently bearing the mistakes of others
- giving good advise to those who need it
- praying to God for the living and dead

Living my faith

Just as your body needs physical nourishment, so your soul needs the nourishment of the Eucharist to grow in holiness and friendship with Christ.

- I'm going to do all I can to go to Communion every day. I'm also going to invite my friends to go and thus help them in their spiritual needs.
- I'm going to carry out the project I drew up with my friends to help those in need.

The Miracles of Jesus
Chapter 4
Review

Match up the columns:

1. Through Creation we can come to know...
2. Man collaborates with God in Creation through his...
3. We call God Creator because he...
4. We say that God is all-powerful because...
5. This virtue makes us trust in God and his promises:
6. Jesus' name means:
7. Peter couldn't stay on top of the water because...
8. Before curing the paralytic, Jesus...
9. To do this is to offend God's love for me:
10. These give birth to many other sins:
11. The two kinds of Works of Mercy are...
12. Everything we do to others...

○ spiritual and corporal

○ sin

○ forgave him his sins

○ nothing is impossible for him

○ capital sins

○ the love, wisdom, goodness and Power of God

○ we do to Christ

○ created everything from nothing

○ "God saves"

○ he became afraid and doubted

○ hope

○ work

Study the following words:

Creation; Hope; Confidence; Trust; Greed; Pride; Laziness; Need

Now fill in the missing letters:

C __ e __ t __ o __; H __ __ e; C __ __ f __ d __ nc __; T __ __ __ __ t; __ __ ee __;

P __ i __ e; L __ __ i __ __ __ __ __; N __ __ d.

Jesus' Friends

Chapter 5

Let Them Come to Me!

Jesus and the Children
Chapter 5, Lesson 1

Remember
Jesus wants you to be his friend.

Now you'll see
Jesus loves you in a very special way.

The Gospel tells us
"And people were bringing children to him that he might touch them, but the disciples rebuked them. When Jesus saw this he became indignant and said to them, *'Let the children come to me; do not prevent them, for the kingdom of God belongs to such as these. Amen, I say to you, whoever does not accept the kingdom of God like a child will not enter it.'* Then he embraced them and blessed them, placing his hands on them."

Mk 10:13-16

Think over the Gospel passage you just read and then answer these questions:

1. Why did the people bring children to Jesus?

2. Why didn't the disciples want the children to get near Jesus?

3. What did Jesus do when he saw what was happening?

4. What did he say to the disciples?

5. What did he do with the children?

6. What does this passage teach you?

Put on a small skit with your classmates, acting out this Gospel passage.

Jesus loves you in a very special way. He showed his love for children in the Gospel when he asked the children to come to him so that he could embrace them and bless them. He didn't care how tired he might have been, or how much work he had ahead of him. He wanted to be with the children. These children of the Gospel represent all the children of the world.

If you had been there, what would you have said to Jesus?

_____

What do you think he would have said in reply?

_____

Why do you think Jesus loves children in a special way?

_____

Children possess two traits that Jesus likes very much. Put the following letters in their correct order and you'll find out what these traits are. Once you've done that, connect each word with its definition.

nercisyti = S __ __ __ __ __ __ __ y

A boy or girl with this trait is always good and kind to others, is joyful and always ready to help others.

donsogse = G __ __ __ __ __ __ s

A boy or girl with this trait always tells the truth, is always honest, and accepts things just as they are.

Find the following words in the alphabet soup below:

children
Jesus
friends
sincerity
goodness

c	h	i	l	d	r	e	n	j
j	a	f	r	i	e	n	d	s
e	h	g	f	d	n	i	o	q
s	g	v	c	d	d	n	u	u
u	x	q	w	a	a	c	q	s
s	i	n	c	e	r	i	t	y
f	d	e	d	e	q	r	a	e
t	r	s	a	q	p	i	z	f
j	h	g	v	c	x	d	y	e
g	o	o	d	n	e	s	s	p
e	q	a	v	g	t	d	m	l

Do you know what this is? _____

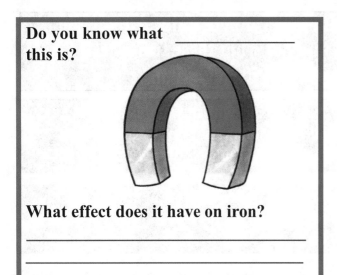

What effect does it have on iron?

_____

_____

A child that is sincere, honest, and good attracts others like a magnet. Others want to be with him or her. A good and honest child will always have lots of friends. What's more, Jesus will be very pleased with him and will always be close to him. That's why this kind of child will also bring other children closer to Jesus.

No doubt you know someone like this among your friends, someone in your class. Write the person's name here and what you like most about him or her.

_____

_____

How can you practice sincerity and honesty?

At home:

_____

At school:

_____

With your friends:

_____

With Jesus:

_____

How can you practice goodness?

At home:

_____

At school:

_____

With your friends:

_____

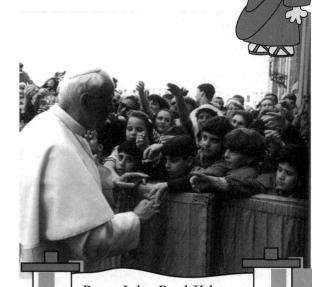

Pope John Paul II loves children a great deal. On his trips all over the world he always takes time to be with children, just as Jesus did.

Now you know how much Jesus loves children.

You can't be with Jesus in the same way the children in the Gospel could, yet Jesus still shows you how much he loves you. One of the ways he does this is through the people in your life.

Under each photo describe what you see in it.

Jesus loves each one of us in a direct, personal, and intense way. In addition to that, however, he also shows us his love in indirect ways, through all the people in our lives, our parents, teachers, friends, priests, etc. Close your eyes and take a few moments to thank Jesus silently for how much he loves you, and ask him for the grace to return that love to him.

Look at the photos and discuss them with your classmates. Connect with a line to Jesus the ones you think he would like.

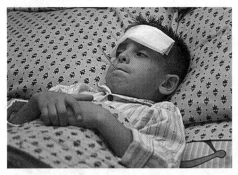

Underline the things you can do to make the world a better place:

- Pray often for children who are in need.
- Take good care of the material things God has given me, aware that a lot of other children don't have such things.
- Think that I deserve everything I have and don't have to share anything. Be selfish!
- Study hard and prepare myself one day to help needy children.
- Be lazy, neglect my homework, only think about taking it easy.
- Live the kind of poverty Jesus invites us to in the Gospel, placing my heart in God and helping others with the material things I have.
- Neglect to take care of my toys, letting them get broken, thinking that my parents will always buy me new ones.
- Be generous in sharing all I have, not just my old, unwanted toys.
- Be aware of the needs of all those around me.

Jesus wants his love to reach children who don't know him yet. You can be the one to show them his love!

Becoming Jesus' friend for the first time

Look at the picture. You already know what's happening in it.

You were born into a Catholic family. When you were still just an infant your parents took you to be baptized.

When were you baptized?
_____

Who took you to be baptized?
_____

Who are your godparents?
_____

What promises did they make on your behalf?
_____

Have you ever renewed those promises? When?
_____

Would you like to have been baptized when you were 10 years old?
_____

Why?
_____

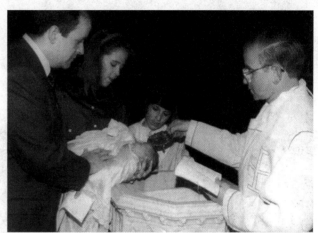

Why do you think people should be baptized when they are still infants? Check off the correct answers:

So that original sin can be wiped from their souls. ◯

Because that's the custom nowadays. ◯

So that they can become children of God as soon as possible and receive Divine Grace. ◯

Because if you wait too long the baptismal gown won't fit anymore. ◯

So that infants can get gifts they need right away. ◯

Because the grace of salvation is for everyone, no matter how old they are. ◯

So that they can be Jesus' friends. ◯

one hundred forty-seven 147

Don't forget

- **Jesus loves children** in a very special way.
- Jesus shows us his love through the different people in our lives.
- Jesus likes very much the virtues of **sincerity** and **goodness** that he sees in children.
- People are baptized as infants to free them from **Original Sin** and so they can be friends of Jesus and **children of God through his grace.**

Knowing my faith

What are the virtues children possess that Jesus likes very much?
Goodness and sincerity (honesty).

Living my faith

Jesus wants to be my friend, and good friends spend time together and talk to one another.

- I'm going to go to the chapel to visit Jesus and talk to him about everything on my mind. I'm going to ask him never to let me stop being his friend.
- I'm going to make a special effort to be sincere, honest, and kind to all those around me since these virtues make Jesus very happy.
- I'm going to do all I can to show other children that Jesus loves them by helping them.
- I'm going to review the project calendar I put together in the last chapter (Lesson 4) to see how well I am living up to my promise to help those in need.

Martha, Martha!

Martha and Mary
Chapter 5, Lesson 2.

Remember
**The First Commandment instructs us to
"Love the Lord your God above all things"**

Now you'll see
**Loving God will make you
immensely happy.**

The Gospel tells us
"As they continued their journey he entered a village where a woman whose name was Martha welcomed him. She had a sister named Mary who sat beside the Lord at his feet listening to him speak. Martha, burdened with much serving, came to him and said, *'Lord, do you not care that my sister has left me by myself to do the serving? Tell her to help me.'* The Lord said to her in reply, *'Martha, Martha, you are anxious and worried about many things. There is need of only one thing. Mary has chosen the better part and it will not be taken from her.'*"

Lk 10:38-42

What was Martha doing?

Read below the different things Martha was doing. Put a check mark to show whether or not each thing was good or bad.

	Good?	Bad?
1. Welcoming guests and attending to them	◯	◯
2. Waiting on guests	◯	◯
3. Preparing Jesus' meal	◯	◯
4. Cleaning the house	◯	◯

But if Martha was doing good things,

What did she do wrong? _____

Why did Jesus answer her the way he did? _____

What does this passage teach us? _____

In your life you spend time doing a lot of good things, and yet Jesus tells us that only one thing is necessary.

Put a red X over the things that are bad, the things you shouldn't do, and write one more bad thing in one of the empty boxes. Draw a blue circle around the good things you should do, and write one more good thing in the other empty box. Draw a green circle around the one thing that is essential.

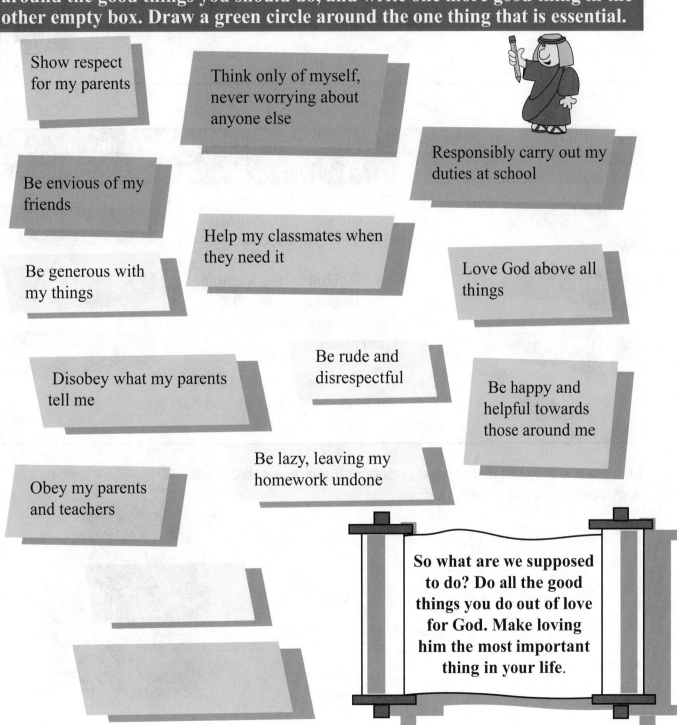

Show respect for my parents

Think only of myself, never worrying about anyone else

Responsibly carry out my duties at school

Be envious of my friends

Help my classmates when they need it

Love God above all things

Be generous with my things

Disobey what my parents tell me

Be rude and disrespectful

Be happy and helpful towards those around me

Obey my parents and teachers

Be lazy, leaving my homework undone

So what are we supposed to do? Do all the good things you do out of love for God. Make loving him the most important thing in your life.

One day, an expert in Jewish Law asked Jesus a question. Look it up in Matthew 22:36 and write down the question here:

_____

_____

What was Jesus' answer? Write it down here:

_____

_____

What does it mean to love God above all things? It has a lot to do with what we call the "theological virtues." Draw lines connecting the three columns:

Believing

Trusting

Loving

Knowing that God's love and assistance will never let us down. Trusting in his justice and mercy.

Knowing that God exists, learning his law, and cultivating our faith. Avoiding anything that might take us away from him.

Building a relationship with God based on sincere love for him and our neighbor.

Charity

Hope

Faith

Love for God should be the most important thing in our lives. And we need to live out that love by:

1. Fulfilling our duties, like Martha.
For example:_____

_____

2. Fulfilling them out of love for God, like Mary.
For example: _____

_____

3. Loving those around me, like Jesus.
For example:_____

_____

What is "Charity"? Fill in the blanks using the words below.

love - God - neighbor - theological - things

Charity is the _____ virtue that enables us to love _____ above all _____, and to love our _____ as ourselves out of _____ for God.

Get your Bible and look up the First Letter of John, chapter 4, verses 20 & 21 in the New Testament. Write the verses out and discuss them with your classmates

_____

_____

_____

You can't see God, but you can see your parents

How do you show them you love them?

_____

What difficulties do you face in showing them your love?

_____

How can you overcome these difficulties?

_____

You can't see God, but you can see your teachers

How do you show them you love them?

_____

What difficulties do you face in showing them your love?

_____

How can you overcome these difficulties?

_____

You can't see God, but you can see your friends

How do you show them you love them?

_____

What difficulties do you face in showing them your love?

_____

How can you overcome these difficulties?

_____

You can't see God, but you can see your siblings

How do you show them you love them?

_____

What difficulties do you face in showing them your love?

_____

How can you overcome these difficulties?

_____

Never forget: you need to love everyone out of love for God.

Look up 1 Corinthians 13:1-3 and copy it down here.

_____

_____

_____

_____

_____

_____

Match up the following descriptions with the person they describe by writing the correct number in each circle.

Does a very good job teaching her students, whom she loves and supports. She spends a lot of time preparing her lessons. ◯

◯ Takes care of his children, making sure they have everything they need.

Loves her children and is always there to help them. Makes sure everything at home is as it should be. ◯

◯ Takes care of and cures those who are sick. Tries to alleviate their pain.

Spends time with people, giving them the sacraments and teaching them about God. ◯

◯ Is very good-hearted, respectful, and obedient, as well as a hard-working student. Always tries his/her best at school. Is well liked by friends.

2 A first-rate mother

1 A first-rate teacher

6 A first-rate me (draw yourself)

5 A first-rate father

3 A first-rate priest

4 A first-rate doctor

St. Paul puts it very clearly: all of these things, without love, are nothing. Only one thing matters: to love God and to love others for his sake.

But what about Mary?

Martha was worried about things that were good, but not the most important. We've just seen that all of these things need to be done out of love for God.
But what was Mary up to all this time?

_____
_____
_____

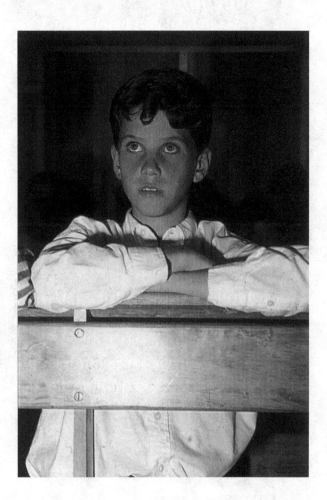

In order to carry out our duties out of love, we must first do what Mary did: sit at the feet of Jesus and listen to him.

Go to the school chapel, taking your catechism book and a pencil with you. Once you're there, try to reconstruct in your mind the scene with Martha and Mary. Place yourself at Jesus' feet and listen to him. After meditating in this way for a few minutes, answer these questions:

What things do you do every day because you have to do them?

_____
_____
_____

How can you do these things in such a way as to show God that you love him?

_____
_____
_____

Before finishing, kneel before Jesus and ask him never to let you break your friendship with him.

Remember
- **Loving God and being Jesus' friend** should be the most important thing in our lives.
- Only by loving God can I be truly **happy.**
- I need to show my love for God by loving others.
- **Charity** is the virtue that enables us to love God above all things, and to love all people out of love for him.

Knowing my faith

What does the First Commandment call us to do?
To believe, trust, and love God above all things.

How can we get to know God better?
Through prayer, reading the Bible, paying close attention at Mass, and making the most of catechism class.

Living my faith
- If I get to know God better my love for him will grow stronger. Thus I'm going to take a few moments every night to read part of the Gospel. I'm also going to remember to visit him in the chapel to ask him to help me love him more.
- My charity towards others will help others to experience God's love for them and make them want to return that love. I'm going to be careful never to speak badly of anyone.
- Out of love for God, I'm going to try to meet this need I see in my class: _____
_____
_____ .

For a mere thirty pieces of silver

Judas, the Friend Turned Traitor
Chapter 5, Lesson 3

Remember
Jesus loves his friends.
Now you'll see
Jesus loves *you* in a very special way.

The Gospel tells us

"Then one of the Twelve, who was called Judas Iscariot, went to the chief priests and said, *'What are you willing to give me if I hand him over to you?'* They paid him thirty pieces of silver, and from that time on he looked for an opportunity to hand him over. His betrayer had arranged a sign with them, saying, *'The man I shall kiss is the one; arrest him.'*

"Immediately he went over to Jesus and said, *'Hail, Rabbi!'* and he kissed him. Jesus answered him, *'Friend, do what you have come for.'* Then stepping forward they laid hands on Jesus and arrested him.

"Then Judas, his betrayer, seeing that Jesus had been condemned, deeply regretted what he had done. He returned the thirty pieces of silver to the chief priests and elders, saying, *'I have sinned in betraying innocent blood.'* They said, *'What is that to us? Look to it yourself.'* Flinging the money into the temple, he departed and went off and hanged himself." **Mt 26:14-16;48-50; 27:3-5**

Name: Judas Iscariot
Birthplace: Kerioth, Judea
Occupation: Disciple of Jesus Christ
Life story: Lived an ordinary life until one day Jesus Christ chose him to be one of his privileged followers. Iscariot witnessed Christ's miracles, listened to his teachings first-hand, and experienced his love. In the end, Iscariot sold his Master for thirty silver pieces. When he realized what was going to happen to Jesus he regretted what he had done. But instead of trusting in the mercy of his friend Jesus, he gave up all hope and lost himself in despair.

The end result is known to all...

Your biography
Name: _____
Birthplace: _____
Occupation: Disciple of Jesus
Life story: Lived an ordinary life until one day Jesus Christ chose him to be one of his privileged followers. He came to know Christ very deeply thanks to the gift of faith he had received at baptism, as well as the example and teachings of the people in his life, his parents, teachers, friends, and priest. He experienced Jesus' love many times in life, especially during difficult moments. Jesus called him to be his apostle, to do great things for God, promising always to be with him in the Eucharist.

This life story could have two very different endings. Pick the one you like most.

He didn't remain faithful to his conscience or his friendship with Christ, which he sold in exchange for money, fame, glory, luxurious living, laziness, selfishness and greed. When he finally realized what he had done, he gave in to despair and refused to listen to his conscience. Then he lost himself in a thousand and one concerns so that he wouldn't be bothered by his conscience. He betrayed the love and mercy of his friend Jesus.
He ended his life in loneliness and despair.

Although he had many chances to betray Jesus, he was faithful to his conscience. He struggled to become a better person every day, even though he had to face a lot of temptations that tried to take him away from his friend Jesus. When things got tough he prayed to Jesus. Even though he fell at times out of weakness, betraying Jesus by sinning, he always trusted in the mercy and love of his friend, seeking his forgiveness in the sacrament of reconciliation. Throughout his life he did all he could to be faithful to his friendship with Jesus and fulfill the will of God.
He was happy all his life, and eventually became a great saint!

Which ending do you like better? Do you think you can get there? How?_____

_____

They are lots of ways for us to find out when things aren't going as they should. Different kinds of signals tell us that something is wrong and needs fixing.

There is also something that lets us know how things are going in our friendship with Jesus, a guide to help us do what is right. Do you know what this thing is? Fill the blanks in its name and definition:

Hello there! I'm the voice of your
C __ N __ C __ E __ C __
Listen carefully to what I have to say!

_____ is the capacity _____ has given us for discerning between _____ and evil and for directing our will towards what is good and away from what is _____.

evil - God - good - Conscience

Study the illustrations. What do you think of the behavior shown in them? Talk it over with your classmates.

Remember that good things are always good, and bad things always bad. To know how to discern between the two we need to form our conscience very well.

What would Jesus have done?

Here are some trustworthy rules for forming your conscience:

1. **Doing something bad in order to achieve something good is never permitted.**
Can you think of an example? Write it down:

_____

_____

2. **The Golden Rule.** Look it up in Matthew 7:12 or Luke 6:31 and write it down here. Then explain it in your own words.

_____

_____

3. **Out of charity, we must respect others and their conscience.**
What would you think of someone who forced another person to do something he or she didn't want to do?

_____

4. **Frequent confession.** This will help you to be in the state of grace. Your friendship with Christ will grow and it will be harder for you to want to break it. Thus you will pay closer attention to your conscience. Finally, the priest's words of advise will help you to form your conscience.

Some things help you follow your conscience, while other things don't. Circle the things that help you follow it and cross out the things that don't.

- Keeping the Commandments

- Stop going to confession

- Obey the teachings of the Church

- Always charitable

- Fight temptation by praying

- Think that nothing is sinful (referred to as a lax conscience)

- Ignore the advise of my parents

- Read the Gospel often and always asking myself, What would Jesus have done in this situation?

- Think that everything is sinful (referred to as a scrupulous conscience, the opposite of a lax one)

Catechism class is very important in this regard. It helps you to know your faith and form your conscience, enabling you to be faithful to Christ all your life. Remember, this is the only thing that will make you truly happy!

- Imitate the good example of others

To follow our conscience, we have to grow accustomed to living by TRUTH.

Look up the following Gospel passages and explain what each one means.

Mt 5:37 _____

Jn 18:37 _____

Jn 8:31-32 _____

Do you remember what the Eighth Commandment is? Write it down here.

_____
_____
_____

The Eighth Commandment calls us to be sincere, not to lie, and not to speak badly about others.

It forbids us from
1. **Telling lies:** that is, deceiving others
2. **Giving false witness:** saying something about another that we know isn't true
3. **Defaming another:** lying in order to damage someone's reputation
4. **Being hypocrites:** seeming to be one thing and really being another
5. **Being vainglorious:** thinking we're better than others because of who we are or what we have

Match the drawings below with the forms of behavior above.
Put an "S" next to the one who is sincere.

"You are great"

"I would like to be his friend"

"I didn't steal it"

"It's her fault"

"I am the best"

"Look at so-and-so?"

Why do people lie?
Think of a lie a child might tell in order to

avoid being punished._____
_____

get something he wants._____
_____

get out of some chore._____
_____

obtain some privilege._____
_____

Draw lines to show what happens to an honest child and one who lies.

- Always takes responsibility for his actions, even when he'd prefer not to.
- People trust him.
- Telling one lie always leads to another.
- He seems to have fewer and fewer friends all the time.
- He's always making new friends.
- He doesn't know what it means to be a friend; he's always bad-mouthing others.
- Thinks he's smarter and better than he really is.
- Is at peace with his conscience.

honest child

child who lies

Countless Christians throughout history have chosen to die rather than betray their faith and live outside the truth. Here are just a few of them. If you know of others tell your classmates about them.

St. Cecilia

St. Stephen

St. Tarsicius

There are many Judases in the world

A lot of people today have turned their backs on Jesus, breaking off their friendship with him through sin. Is there anything you can do about this?

1. What you can do for yourself:

• Pray every day, asking God to help you be **faithful to your conscience**. Remember that in the Our Father we ask God to "lead us not into temptation."

• Being faithful to your conscience will mean waging a daily battle. **Prayer** is the key to winning this battle. If you remain watchful and close to God, you will always be able to hear the voice of your conscience.

• Go to **confession** often, taking time carefully to **examine your conscience** beforehand, asking God to help you. And do your best to put into practice the **advise** the priest gives you.

2. What you can do for others:

• Pray before the Eucharist to help make reparation for the sins people commit.

• Offer up to Jesus all the good you do as a way to counteract all the evil in the world. You can do this as you pray your morning offering, and then renew it at Mass and during your visits to the chapel.

• Pray a lot for the spiritual needs of people everywhere so that God will help them to be his faithful friends so everyone may know what you already know: Christ is the only source of true happiness.

• Put together a little schedule for praying so that you won't forget to pray every day.

• Always provide others with a good example.

• Show love and kindness towards others. That will help them draw closer to Jesus.

Don't forget

- Jesus is your friend, and he wants you to be his faithful friend.
- To be faithful to Jesus you have to be faithful to your conscience.
- You need to live in the truth and never lie.
- You can help make reparation for the sins of others by praying to Christ in the Eucharist.

Knowing my faith

What is the Eighth Commandment?
"You shall not lie or bear false witness."
What does this Commandment tell us?
To be honest and never to lie.
What does it mean to lie?
To say something we know to be untrue, with the intention of deceiving someone.
What is conscience?
It is the capacity God has given us to discern between good and evil and to direct our will towards good and away from evil.
What does man's conscience instruct him to do?
To do good and avoid evil.

Living my faith

- I'm going to do my morning offering every day and thus make reparation for the sins committed against the Sacred Heart of Jesus.
- I'm going to go to confession, examining myself especially on how I've kept the Eighth Commandment faithful to my conscience.
- I'm going to offer my morning offering for the following intentions this week:

Monday:_____
Tuesday: _____
Wednesday: _____
Thursday: _____ (Thursdays are dedicated to the Eucharist and the reparation of sins.)
Friday: _____
Saturday: _____ (Saturdays are dedicated to Mary; offer your prayer to her.)
Sunday: _____

Come Down From There!

Zacchaeus
Chapter 5, Lesson 4

Remember
your greatest treasure is your friendship with Christ.

Now you'll see
Jesus seeks out sinners to make them his friends again.

The Gospel tells us

"He came to Jericho and intended to pass through the town. Now a man there named Zacchaeus, who was a chief tax collector and also a wealthy man, was seeking to see who Jesus was; but he could not see him because of the crowd, for he was short in stature. So he ran ahead and climbed a sycamore tree in order to see Jesus, who was about to pass that way. When he reached the place, Jesus looked up and said to him, *'Zacchaeus, come down quickly, for today I must stay at your house.'* And he came down quickly and received him with joy. When they all saw this, they began to grumble, saying, *'He has gone to stay at the house of a sinner.'* But Zacchaeus stood there and said to the Lord, *'Behold, half of my possessions, Lord, I shall give to the poor, and if I have extorted anything from anyone I shall repay it four times over.'* And Jesus said to him, *'Today salvation has come to this house because this man too is a descendant of Abraham. For the Son of Man has come to seek and to save what was lost.'"*

Lk 19:1-10

Answer the following questions:

What kind of person was Zacchaeus?_____
_____

If Zacchaeus was so important, why did he want to see Jesus so badly that he climbed a tree to do so?

_____

With so many people around, why did Jesus pick him?

_____
_____

Why did Jesus want to eat in Zacchaeus' house? There must have been more important people in Jericho.

_____

What did Zacchaeus say to Jesus? What did this mean for Zacchaeus?_____
_____

What did Jesus mean by this?_____
_____

What kind of salvation was Jesus talking about?_____

_____

How do you think Zacchaeus lived after his conversion?_____

_____
_____

Who was this man Zacchaeus?

He was a rich man, in charge of those who collected taxes from the Jews for the Romans. His fellow Jews didn't like him because he helped the Romans, and often cheated and imposed heavier taxes than he should have.

Do you remember what the Seventh Commandment is? Write it down here.

What did Zacchaeus do to break the Seventh Commandment?

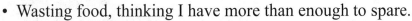

There is another way of breaking the Seventh Commandment.

Wasting things (food, water, electricity) and spending more than one needs to spend.
Read the following sentences and reflect on them.

• Wasting food, thinking I have more than enough to spare.
• Buying everything that catches my eye, even though I don't need it.
• Getting mad at my parents when they won't buy me something I want.
• Letting water go to waste since I know we'll never run out at my house.
• Making no effort to take care of my games and toys.
• Not taking care of my school materials since I know I'll be given new ones if they get damaged or lost.

Tips for overcoming these kinds of attitudes.
• When money is given to you, don't spend all of it if you don't need to, and be sure to share with those who have less.
• Get used to making small sacrifices, putting up with heat, hunger or tiredness without complaining.
• Take care of your things, seeing them as gifts from God to help you be a better person.
• Thank God for what you have instead of complaining about what you don't have.

How do I spend my money?

On your own, without saying anything to anyone else, think back over the past week and ask yourself, What have I spent my money on? What have others bought for me? Did I really need those things, or could I have gotten by without them?

On a separate sheet make a list of all your toys. It could be that you don't need a lot of them and play with them rarely. Perhaps you could underline some toys you could give to other children who have very few or no toys at all.

Look up Matthew 6:21.

Where was Zacchaeus' heart?

Before he knew Jesus.

His heart was tied up in collecting a lot of taxes and making himself very wealthy, even if it meant stealing.

After he knew Jesus.

His heart was committed to making up for the damage he had done (called reparation) and following Christ, living out his teachings, loving his neighbor, and becoming a saint.

If I have cheated anyone

Zacchaeus made up for the evil he had committed by making restitution (returning stolen goods or paying the owner their value). His conversion of heart was total, even though it most certainly meant giving up a lot of things.

He embraced a true **spirit of reparation** for the evil he had done.

Write a brief paragraph describing Zacchaeus' life after his conversion.

Zacchaeus, Chief Tax Collector

_____
_____
_____
_____
_____
_____
_____
_____

Do you remember the five steps to a good confession?

Write them down here:

1. _____.
Which means:_____
2. _____
Which means:_____
3. _____
Which means:_____
4. _____
Which means:_____
5. _____
Which means:_____

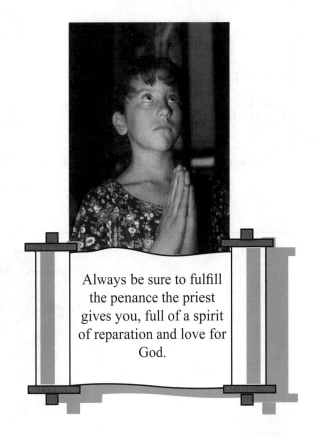

Always be sure to fulfill the penance the priest gives you, full of a spirit of reparation and love for God.

When the priest assigns you a penance in confession, he gives you the chance to make up for the offenses against God's love that you have committed by sinning.

Yet some sins wound our neighbor or cause him some kind of damage. Such sins are forgiven in confession, but the damage they have done is not repaired. This is when we must say to Jesus, together with Zacchaeus:

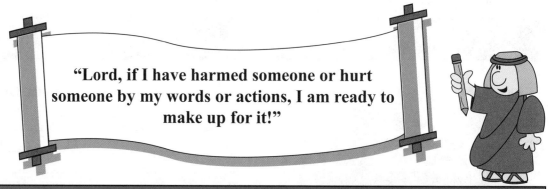

"Lord, if I have harmed someone or hurt someone by my words or actions, I am ready to make up for it!"

Below write down how you think someone should make reparation when he has sinned by.

- telling a lie about a classmate.

- making fun of someone.

- disobeying and thus bringing harm on others.

- carelessly breaking his brother's toy.

- hitting his little brother for "acting like a baby."

- thinking himself better than others and so being mean to them.

- taking something that isn't his.

Other ways to make up for our sins

Praying

Offerings

Making sacrifices

Works of mercy

Helping others

And also through your morning offering every day:

Offer up to God everything you're going to do during the day, and then put lots of effort into doing them the best you can and out of love for God. This, too, is a way to make up for the sins and offenses against love that you have committed.

Don't forget

- Jesus wants very much to have all people be his friends and that's why he seeks out sinners to help them repent and return to him.
- Friendship with Christ is stronger than any sin.
- We should strive to make up for the damage caused by our sins and fulfill the penances we receive.
- Excessive spending and letting things go to waste are faults against the Seventh Commandment.

Knowing my faith

What is the Seventh Commandment?
"You shall not steal."

What is the Tenth Commandment?
"You shall not covet your neighbor's goods."

Living my faith

- Zacchaeus did everything he could to meet Jesus. I'm going to go to the chapel and ask Jesus, my best friend, to call me back to him if I ever happen to turn away from him.
- As a sacrifice of reparation for my sins, I'm going to embrace Gospel poverty throughout this week: taking care of my things, not buying anything I don't really need, and helping others in any way I can.
- I'm going to pray my morning offering every day.

Jesus' Friends
Chapter 5
Review

Match up the two columns.

1. Qualities of children that Jesus likes:

2. Jesus shows us his love through...

3. People are baptized as infants so they...

4. The one essential thing in life is to...

5. Loving God means three things:

6. We should perform good deeds...

7. God's voice in our souls:

8. The Eighth Commandment instructs us...

9. Being a hypocrite means...

10. The Seventh Commandment instructs us...

11. Excessive spending and waste are faults...

12. An excessive desire for wealth is called...

○ the people around us

○ love God above all things

○ greed

○ conscience

○ not to lie or give false witness

○ believing, trusting, loving

○ out of love for God

○ sincerity and goodness

○ seeming to be one thing and being another

○ against the Seventh Commandment

○ not to steal

○ can be children of God and friends of Jesus.

Study the following words:

Sincerity; Hypocrisy; Conscience; Poverty; Betrayal; Covet

Now fill in the missing letters:

Sin __ er __ ty; H __ p __ cr __ s __; C __ n __ c ___ nc __; __ o __ ert __; __ e __ r __ y __ l; C __ v __ t.

The Last Supper

Chapter 6

Who's Most Important?

The Places of Honor
Chapter 6, Lesson 1

Remember
**Jesus taught us that serving
others is the way to salvation.**

Now you'll see
**we need to pause every once in a while
to make sure we're on the right track.**

The Gospel tells us

"Then an argument broke out among the disciples about which of them should be regarded as the greatest. He said to them, *'The kings of the Gentiles lord it over them and those in authority over them are addressed as "Benefactors"; but among you it shall not be so. Rather, let the greatest among you be as the youngest, and the leader as the servant. For who is greater: the one seated at table or the one who serves? Is it not the one seated at table? I am among you as the one who serves. It is you who have stood by me in my trials; and I confer a kingdom on you, just as my Father has conferred one on me, that you may eat and drink at my table in my kingdom; and you will sit on thrones judging the twelve tribes of Israel.'"*

Lk 22:24-30

"I am among you as one who serves"

Color in the circles next to the sentences that show Jesus came to serve others.

◯ Jesus came to earth to save man from sin.

◯ Jesus came to earth because he needed a vacation.

◯ Jesus died to save us.

◯ Jesus taught us the true way to live.

◯ Jesus came to become famous through his miracles.

◯ Jesus healed the sick.

◯ Jesus forgave sinners.

Jesus, though he was God, became man to serve mankind.

Different kinds of greatness

For many people, the greatest person is the one who

• has power, orders others, and commands others to obey him or her.
• is very rich and can have whatever he or she wants.
• is very famous and praised by everyone.

For God, the greatest person is the one who

• serves others with joy.
• doesn't want anything beyond what he or she really needs.
• spends his or her life doing good deeds no one sees or knows about.

Which of these children think as God thinks, and which ones think as people think?

1 "When I grow up I'm going to collect sports cars!"

2 "I'm going to be an actress and become very famous."

3 "I'm going to help my mother without letting anyone realize it."

4 "I'm going to share everything I have with those who have very little."

5 "I like to order people around and have them obey me."

6 "I like to find out what other people need so I can help them."

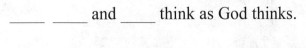
____, ____ and ____ think as God thinks.

____, ____ and ____ think as people think.

Only God can make a person truly happy

Have you noticed that people usually think they'll be happy getting some material thing, only to find out once they have it that they want something else or something more?

"I finally got the car I needed. But now there's a new one out with a convertible top and wide tires. If I could get one of those I'd be really happy."

"I've got the house I always wanted, but now I wish it had a pool and fitness center. That's what would make me truly happy."

"They finally bought me the doll I wanted. But now I need the doll house and clothes, and things that go with it. When I get those I'll be happy once and for all!"

"I finally got the video game I kept asking for. But now there's a new one that's even better. When I get that one I'll be really happy."

Throughout history, people of every period and every culture have realized that nothing in this world can make them completely happy. That's because God has placed in our hearts a longing for supernatural happiness, a longing that can't be met by all the money in the world, all the fame in the world, or all the power in the world. Only God can fill that longing. All the ancient cultures had their own gods, which shows man's desire to be with God.

"I am Zeus, god of the Greeks."

"I am Quetzalcoatl, god of the Aztecs."

"I'm Jupiter, god of the Romans."

"I am Kukulkan, god of the Maya."

"I am Yahweh, the True God, Creator of heaven and earth."

"I'm Ra, god of the Egyptians."

Man will always be unsatisfied until he possesses God fully in heaven. As St. Augustine once wrote.

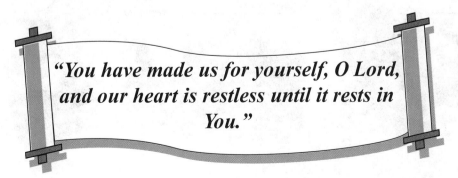

"You have made us for yourself, O Lord, and our heart is restless until it rests in You."

Jesus is the way

If God is the only thing that can make us happy, what do we have to do to find him?
God the Father sent us Jesus to save us from sin. He also sent him to teach us how to live.
Jesus is the perfect man. He invites us to be his disciples, to follow him, and imitate him.
Through his life, Jesus teaches us to love others by serving them.
Jesus himself once said:

"The Son of man has not come to be served, but to serve and to give his life for others."
(Mt 20:28)

He also said:

"I am the Way, the Truth and the Life. No one comes to the Father except through me."
(Jn. 14:6)

How can I serve others in order to imitate Jesus?

Look at the following scenes and circle the children who are serving others.

Imitating Jesus is not easy

Do you remember the capital sins (Chapter 4, Lesson 4)? They are your main enemies in imitating Jesus by serving others.

Find the names of these seven sins in this alphabet soup:

p	r	i	d	e	b	i	a	u	l
g	u	l	a	f	i	a	f	o	u
a	g	l	u	t	t	o	n	y	s
g	r	c	a	n	g	e	r	p	t
o	a	e	n	v	y	d	i	a	r
f	d	s	e	w	a	d	c	p	i
m	s	s	e	n	i	z	a	l	a
a	v	g	r	e	e	d	a	x	z

Write the name of each capital sin next to its definition:

1 _____ Thinking you're better than others, that others are nothing in comparison with you.

2 _____ Wanting to have more and more things, just to have them, and never sharing with anybody.

3 _____ Feeling bitter or sad when someone is better than you or has things you don't.

4 _____ Losing your temper to the point of hurting others verbally or physically.

5 _____ Degrading the idea of love with selfish desires. Also includes selfish and excessive desire to experience bodily pleasures: caresses, comforts, etc.

6 _____ Letting yourself be taken over by an immoderate longing for food or drink, even to the point of doing yourself harm.

7 _____ Taking things as easy as possible, neglecting your duties. Shunning anything that takes effort.

There are certain attitudes, or ways of living, that will enable you to easily overcome these capital sins. But they are attitudes you must sow and cultivate within you.

To combat pride, Humility
To combat greed, Magnanimity
To combat anger, Patience
To combat envy, Generosity
To combat lust, Chastity
To combat gluttony, Temperance
To combat laziness, Diligence

Trace the path to happiness below. Whenever you come up against a capital sin, write above it the name of the attitude that conquers it so that you'll be able to keep advancing.

If you don't want to lose your way, STOP to check your map.

The capital sins are not your only challenge on the road to happiness. There are also side roads you can accidentally go down and end up losing your way. So you need to keep your eyes open and stop every once in a while to check to make sure you're on the right road.

It's best to take a few minutes every night, before going to bed, to check to make sure you're on the right road.

Use this as a guide for checking your progress.

- *Ask the Holy Spirit to help you, to enlighten you to see things clearly, just as they are.*
- *Remember that God is everywhere, and beside you at this moment.*
- *Thank him for all that he has given you: your life, your body, your parents, friends, and all the good things that have happened to you today.*
- *Examine your actions and attitudes today: both good and bad, and place them before God.*
- *Offer to God all the good things that have happened during the day. Renew your desire to be holy and to be his friend, helping him to make the world a better place.*
- *Ask his forgiveness for the sins, faults or mistakes you've committed today.*
- *Finish by making a resolution to correct tomorrow anything you might have done wrong today.*

It's essential that this examination not become *a mere listing of sins committed* in the course of your day. Rather, it should be a way of monitoring your progress and detecting any setbacks so as to resume pursuing your goals and become a better person every day.

The following questions can help you do your nightly exam.

As a son or daughter:
Have I been obedient to my parents?
Have I shown respect in speaking to them?
Have I helped whenever they asked me to?

As a brother or sister:
Have I fought with my brothers or sisters?
Have I shared my things with them?
Have I done my best to help them whenever I could?

As a friend:
Have I been a good friend today?
Did I follow all the rules when I played?
Did I lie, cheat, or make fun of anyone?

As a student:
Did I pay attention in all my classes?
Did I do my homework with diligence and thoroughness?
Did I break any school rules?

In my prayers:
Did I spend some time in prayer today?
Did I remember to offer all my activities to God?
Did I receive Jesus in Holy Communion?

Don't forget

- Nothing in this world can totally and definitively satisfy the human person.
- True happiness is found only in God.
- God has shown us the way to him in his Son Jesus.
- Jesus has taught us that serving others is the way to God.
- The capital sins are our enemies in seeking to serve others.
- We can overcome the capital sins by developing attitudes that are their opposites.
- I ought to do a daily examination of conscience at the end of the day and make a resolution for the following day.

Knowing my faith

What is the purpose of the daily examination of conscience?
To check to make sure we are on the right road and to get back on it if we have strayed.

What are the steps to making a good daily examination of conscience?
There are six steps:
1. Invoke God's help, reminding myself that I am in his presence.
2. Thank him for all that he has given me during the day.
3. Examine my day, together with him, seeing both the good and the bad.
4. Offer to him the good things, telling him I want to be his friend.
5. Ask his forgiveness for any bad things I have done.
6. Make a resolution for the following day.

Living my faith

- This week I'm going to do my best to anticipate the wishes and needs of my parents, teachers, relatives, and friends, offering to help them before they have to ask.
- I'm going to do my examination of conscience every night so I do not lose my way on the road Jesus has taught me to follow.

How Could I Ever Let Him?

Jesus Washes his Disciples' Feet
Chapter 6, Lesson 2

Remember
esus left us a New Commandment.

Now you're going to s...
Jesus left us certain signs to continue showing us his love for us.

The Gospel tells us

"Before the feast of Passover, Jesus knew that his hour had come to pass from this world to the Father. He loved his own in the world and he loved them to the end. The devil had already induced Judas, son of Simon the Iscariot, to hand him over. So, during supper, fully aware that the Father had put everything into his power and that he had come from God and was returning to God, he rose from supper and took off his outer garments. He took a towel and tied it around his waist. Then he poured water into a basin and began to wash the disciples' feet and dry them with the towel around his waist. He came to Simon Peter, who said to him, *'Master, are you going to wash my feet?'* Jesus answered and said to him, *'What I am doing, you do not understand now, but you will understand later.'* Peter said to him, *'You will never wash my feet.'* Jesus answered him, *'Unless I wash you, you will have no inheritance with me.'* Simon Peter said to him, *'Master, then not only my feet, but my hands and head as well.'* Jesus said to him, *'Whoever has bathed has no need except to have his feet washed, for he is clean all over; so you are clean, but not all.'* For he knew who would betray him; for this reason, he said, *'Not all of you are clean.'* So when he had washed their feet and put his garments back on and reclined at table again, he said to them, *'Do you realize what I have done for you? You call me "teacher" and "master," and rightly so, for indeed I am. If I, therefore, the master and teacher, have washed your feet, you ought to wash one another's feet. I have given you a model to follow, so that as I have done for you, you should also do.'*

"When he [Judas] had left, Jesus said, *'Now is the Son of Man glorified, and God is glorified in him. If God is glorified in him, God will also glorify him in himself, and he will glorify him at once. My children, I will be with you only a little while longer. You will look for me, and as I told the Jews, "Where I go you cannot come," so now I say it to you. I give you a new commandment: love one another. As I have loved you, so you also should love one another. This is how all will know that you are my disciples, if you have love for one another.'*"

Jn 13:1-5; 31-35

Answer the following questions.

What did Jesus do during the Last Supper to teach the disciples that serving others is the way to salvation?

_____

_____

Why do you think Peter didn't want Jesus to wash his feet?

_____

_____

What was the New Commandment that Jesus gave his disciples?

_____

_____

_____

What did Jesus say about how we would be recognized as his disciples?

_____

Never forget

Jesus became man to serve men. He had nothing to gain from it. His great LOVE for each one of us is what drove him to do it.

He knew that we were sick, and he came to cure us. He knew that we were in darkness, and he came to bring us light. Jesus wanted to reconcile us with God, he wanted us to know the LOVE of God. He wanted to share with us his Divine Nature and wanted to show us the way to Life by becoming our model.

That's why, even though he was God, Jesus chose to become a true man together with all that being a man meant. He took on a human body, a human soul, human intelligence, and a human will. This means that Jesus thought as you think, felt as you feel, suffered, and had to struggle just as you do.

What is "Love"?

In his first Letter to the Corinthians, St. Paul left us a beautiful description of love, one that can help you very much as you strive to keep Jesus' New Commandment.

"Love is always patient and kind; it is never jealous; love is never boastful or conceited; it is never rude or selfish; it does not take offense, and is not resentful. Love takes no pleasure in other people's sins but delights in the truth; it is always ready to excuse, to trust, to hope, and to endure whatever comes."

Read the following boxes. If the box contains a characteristic of love according to St. Paul's letter, put a green circle around it. If it doesn't, put a red circle around it.

Be patient. Know how to wait without being demanded.

Be helpful. Help others whenever they need it.

Be envious. Be bitter because someone else is better than you.

Be kind. Always think and speak well of others.

Be conceited. Tell others about the good things I've done and how great I am.

Be on the lookout for what is best for me.

Be impolite. Be rude or indifferent to others.

Bear grudges towards those who wrong me in any way.

Be touchy, ready to lash out at anyone who bothers me.

Rejoice when others are treated unfairly. Smile and laugh when things go badly for someone else.

Rejoice in the truth. Never cheat or lie to get ahead. Know how to win or lose with joy.

Always forgive others. Be understanding, forgetting any evil others do to me.

Be trusting. Be ready to believe as true what others tell me.

Never give up hoping. Realize that people can change. Think that others want to be better people every day.

Be patient. Don't complain about things; know how to put up with suffering and hardship, when necessary.

Find in the newspaper two news items: one that speaks of love and another that speaks of selfishness. Paste them here and write what you think about them:

Love	Selfishness

What I think: _____

_____
_____
_____
_____
_____
_____

What I think: _____

_____
_____
_____
_____
_____
_____

List here some ways you can live Jesus' commandment of love in your family, choosing three characteristics of love from St. Paul's Letter to the Corinthians. Follow the example given.

Characteristic: *Be patient.*
With my parents: *Waiting for them to finish speaking before speaking myself.*
With my brothers and sisters: *Wating for my brother to finish using the bathroom, without shouting or banging on the door.*

Characteristic: _____
With my parents: _____

With my brothers and sisters:_____

Characteristic: _____
With my parents:_____

With my brothers and sisters:_____

Characteristic: _____
With my parents:_____

With my brothers and sisters:_____

Jesus shows us his love for us through the sacraments.

Everyday, we make use of many signs, or symbols, to express ideas, feelings, and other such things. For example:
• We shake hands or embrace to show that we have forgiven someone.
• We give our mother a kiss to show her we love her.
• We stand up to greet someone as a sign of respect.

Jesus used signs, too, to show us his great love for us. He helps us by sending us special graces through the signs we call the sacraments.

Pay very close attention as you read the following.

The sacraments are **signs** that Jesus established and entrusted to the Church. His purpose in doing so was to give us special graces that would help us on the road to salvation.

There are seven sacraments:

• Baptism
This sacrament initiates us into the life of the Church and the life of faith. It cleanses us of Original Sin, makes us children of God, and members of the Church.

• Confirmation
This sacrament gives us special strength to build up the faith we received at baptism. Through it we receive the Holy Spirit and commit ourselves to being Christ's witnesses in the world, becoming soldiers of Christ and the Church.

• Eucharist
In this sacrament we recall and renew Christ's sacrifice. Bread and wine become the Body and Blood of Christ so as to become the nourishment of our souls.

• Penance and Reconciliation

This is the sacrament Christ uses to bring us back into the life of grace by forgiving us our sins.

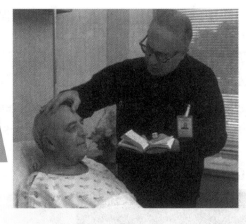

• Anointing of the sick

The purpose of this sacrament is to give special graces of peace, consolation, and fortitude to those suffering grave illness or old age.

•Holy Orders

In this sacrament Christ makes certain men he has chosen into ministers of the Church, giving them the graces they need to carry out their mission.

•Matrimony

Through this sacrament Christ blesses the union of a man and a woman, giving them special graces to be faithful in their love for one another.

The sacraments are God's masterpiece in his longing to help man. The holiness of the one who administers the sacrament doesn't matter. God always gives us sacramental grace through them, no matter what; that's why we say the sacraments are "efficacious."

The sacraments are extremely helpful gifts from God. Their effects help the one who receives them: sanctifying him and building up his faith, as well as the entire Church, making it stronger. For this reason the sacraments are said to bear both **personal fruits** and **ecclesial fruits.**

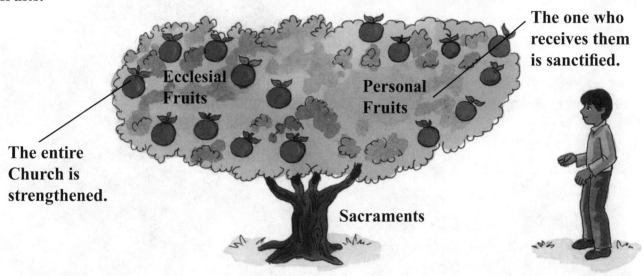

The one who receives them is sanctified.

Ecclesial Fruits

Personal Fruits

The entire Church is strengthened.

Sacraments

To help you understand how the entire Church is strengthened when just one Catholic Christian receives the sacraments, do the following experiment. Get four paper cups and a straw. Cut holes in the cups and cut up the straw, putting them together like this:

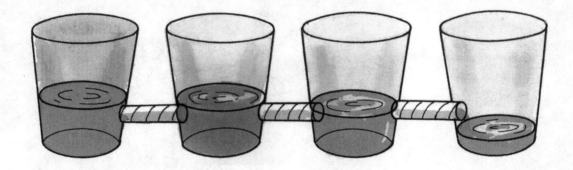

Now fill up one of the cups with colored water. See what happens? They all get filled! The Church is like a network of inter-connected cups. God gives his grace to one, and everyone benefits!

Don't forget

• Jesus showed us his love for us by becoming a man to save us.
• Jesus left us a New Commandment, the commandment of love.
• Jesus continues to show us his love through the sacraments.

Knowing my faith

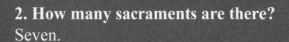

1. What are the sacraments?
They are signs Jesus left to help us gain salvation.

2. How many sacraments are there?
Seven.

3. Name the sacraments.
Baptism, Confirmation, The Eucharist, Penance and Reconciliation, Anointing of the Sick, Holy Orders, Matrimony.

4. What purpose do the sacraments serve?
The sacraments achieve three things: they sanctify individuals, build up the Church, and increase our faith.

Living my faith

• This week I'm not going to pass up any opportunity to receive Jesus in Communion every day and to thank him for the gift of the sacraments.
• I'm going to keep in mind that love for others was the road to salvation that Jesus taught us. I'm going to show this love for my family by putting into practice the things I wrote on page 190.

The Greatest of Gifts

Jesus Institutes the Eucharist
Chapter 6, Lesson 3

Remember
Jesus continues to be with us.
Now your going to see
God's love for man is tender and affectionate.

The Gospel tells us

"While they were eating, Jesus took bread, said the blessing, broke it, and giving it to his disciples said,

'Take this all of you and eat it. This is my body, which will be given up for you.'

Then he took a cup, gave thanks, and gave it to them, saying,

'Take this all of you and drink from it. This is my blood, the blood of the new and everlasting covenant. It will be shed for you and for all so that sins may be forgiven. Do this in memory of me'."

Mt 26:26-28

Reflection

Jesus wanted to stay with us forever to help us and guide us on the road to salvation. He was and is God Almighty. He could have stayed with us in any way he liked. He could, for example, have stayed with us in the form of a huge statue with magical powers to save and sanctify anyone who touched it. He could have given the statue magnetic powers to draw all men to it. He could have, but he didn't.

His love for us is so sensitive that he didn't want anything too spectacular that might take away our full freedom in approaching him. Jesus chose the most simple of ways, the most common and regular. He chose to remain with us in a piece of bread. Bread is a symbol of nourishment. By choosing bread, Jesus wanted us to realize that the Eucharist is the nourishment of our souls, the food that makes our souls grow and be strong.

The gift of a friend as he says good-bye

Imagine that you and your family are getting ready to go live in another country. You get together with your best friends one last time, knowing that you won't be seeing them anymore. What would you give them as a gift so they would have something to remember you by? Write it down here:

_____

_____

How would you want your friends to treat the gift you gave them?

Underline the sentences that express how you would like them to treat it.

- Let it get buried in a drawer under other things so that sooner or later they'd forget about you.

- Throw it in the garbage.

- Put it in a special place to take out now and then to think of you.

- Throw on the ground, step on it, and break it.

- Keep it with them always so that they would think of you everyday.

> **Jesus Christ is really and truly present in the Eucharist**

God's love for us is so great that it didn't stop at becoming a man for us. In the Eucharist, **God conceals himself in a fragile piece of bread** to feed man, inviting us to share in his own divine life.

God, the All-powerful One, sacrifices, or sets aside, all his power and makes himself accessible to anyone who wants to receive him in the Eucharist.

This sacrifice is repeated every time we celebrate Holy Mass.

BREAD AND WINE ---- **CONSECRATION TRANSUBSTANTATION** ---- **BODY AND BLOOD OF CHRIST**

Jesus talks to us about the Eucharist

Divide into small groups. Study the following phrases from the Gospel and discuss their meaning. Once you have reached an agreement as a group, write down the meaning on the lines provided.

"I am the bread of life"

_____

_____

_____

"He who eats my flesh and drinks my blood will abide in me and I in him"

_____

_____

_____

"If anyone eats this bread he will live forever"

_____

_____

_____

"If you do not eat the flesh of the Son of Man and drink his blood, you will not have life within you"

_____

_____

_____

A very important person

Imagine that someone very important has invited you to his or her house: the Pope, the president, your favorite actress, athlete or singer. Put a check mark after the action you think you would do.

Before going over to his or her house I would:
• not do anything special to get ready _____
• put on my best outfit and comb my hair _____
• do something else _____

When it came time to talk to him or her, I would:
• speak with respect, gratitude, and admiration _____
• talk the same way I talk to everyone else _____
• show disrespect _____

What can I do to thank Jesus for wanting to stay with us?

Keep in mind:
- Jesus is far more important than any other human person, no matter how famous he or she might be.
- Jesus is really present in the Eucharist.
- Jesus is your friend and left you the Eucharist as a gift.
- God himself became food for you, out of love for you, so that you might become one with him

Carefully consider the following things you could do and ask yourself whether they would be go ways to respond to the love Jesus shows you in the Eucharist.

• Cultivate my prayer-life
Go often to visit Jesus in the Eucharist, speaking with him as I would with the closest of friends, and show him my gratitude and love.

• Adore Christ in the Eucharist (Eucharistic Adoption)
The Eucharist is God himself under the appearances of bread and wine. Kneeling before Jesus in the Blessed Sacrament, I will maintain an attitude of respect and reverence. I will worship him as God, as the Creator of all things, the Lord of my entire life and, the one who has given me all that I have and am.

• Unite myself to his sacrifice in the Mass
He sacrifices his greatness to become my nourishment, to become one with me. I should place my life on the paten, offering to him all that I am and have so that I can be united to him forever. I will do everything I can to receive him in Communion every day, even if it doesn't fit into my schedule easily.

• Keep the promises I have made
Jesus has always been a faithful friend to me and I need to treat him in the same way. I need to do all I can to keep the promises I made to him at baptism and renewed at my First Communion.

> **What do you think of these four ways of thanking Jesus for the gift of the Eucharist? Would you eliminate one of them? Would you add others?**
>
> _____
>
> _____
>
> _____
>
> _____

Do you remember the effects Holy Communion has on your soul?

Match up the two columns by drawing a line between the effects of Communion and their meanings.

The effects of Communion	Meaning
• Deepens our union with Christ and the Church.	• Makes us closer friends of Jesus.
• Grants forgiveness of our venial sins.	• As closer friends of Jesus, he forgives for the small faults we have committed against him.
• Protects us from mortal sin.	• Since we become better friends of Jesus, we try to stay away from mortal sin.

Fill in the missing word of the Church's Third Precept.

"You shall receive _____ at least during the Easter Season."

Because of the magnificent effects of Communion, the Church encourages us to receive Communion frequently, every time we go to Mass.

There are two conditions for being able to receive Holy Communion:

• To be in friendship with God, in a state of grace, without any mortal sins that haven't been forgiven in confession.

• To fast for one hour before receiving Communion.

Learn the following prayer and say it whenever you want to receive Christ in Communion, but, for some reason, cannot.

Oh my Jesus, I believe that you are really present in the Blessed Sacrament of the Altar. I love you above all things and long to receive you into my soul. But since I can't receive you sacramentally right now, at least come spiritually into my heart. Stay with me forever and never let me be separated from you. Amen.

Don't forget

- At the Last Supper Jesus instituted the sacrament of the Eucharist so he could remain with us forever.
- In the Eucharist, God Almighty conceals himself in a fragile piece of bread out of love for us, to be our food and to strengthen our souls.
- God repeats this act of loving sacrifice every time Mass is celebrated.
- We need to thank God for this sacrifice of infinite love by praying to him, adoring him, offering sacrifices to him, and keeping the promises we have made to him.

Knowing your faith

1. When did Christ institute the Eucharist?
At the Last Supper.

2. What is the Eucharist?
It is the sacrament in which bread and wine become the Body and Blood of Jesus Christ.

3. What are the conditions for receiving Holy Communion?
To be in friendship with God and to have fasted for one hour.

4. What are the effects of Holy Communion?
It unites us more closely to Christ and the Church, gives forgiveness of venial sins, and helps us not to fall into mortal sin.

5. Why should we visit Jesus in the Eucharist?
Because it gives us the chance to show him our gratitude, love, and adoration.

Living my faith

- I'm going to visit Jesus in the Blessed Sacrament to tell him how grateful I am to him for wanting to remain with me.
- On Sunday, before going to Mass, I'm going to tell my family about what I learned today so that we will prepare ourselves well to receive Jesus in Holy Communion.

Without Me, You Can Do Nothing

Words at the Last Supper
Chapter 6, Lesson 4

Remember

if you keep the Commandments you'll be Jesus' friend.

Now you'll see

there are certain things you have to do to be a good friend.

The Gospel tells us

"When the supper was over, Jesus said to his disciples, *'I am the true vine, and my Father is the vine grower. He takes away every branch in me that does not bear fruit, and everyone that does he prunes so that it bears more fruit. You are already pruned because of the word that I spoke to you. Remain in me, as I remain in you. Just as a branch cannot bear fruit on its own unless it remains on the vine, so neither can you unless you remain in me. I am the vine, you are the branches. Whoever remains in me and I in him will bear much fruit, because without me you can do nothing. Anyone who does not remain in me will be thrown out like a branch and wither; people will gather them and throw them into a fire and they will be burned. If you remain in me and my words remain in you, ask for whatever you want and it will be done for you. By this is my Father glorified, that you bear much fruit and become my disciples. 'As the Father loves me, so I also love you. Remain in my love. If you keep my commandments, you will remain in my love, just as I have kept my Father's commandments and remain in his love. I have told you this so that my joy may be in you and your joy may be complete. This is my commandment: love one another as I love you. No one has greater love than this, to lay down one's life for one's friends. You are my friends if you do what I command you. I no longer call you slaves, because a slave does not know what his master is doing. I have called you friends, because I have told you everything I have heard from my Father. It was not you who chose me, but I who chose you and appointed you to go and bear fruit that will remain, so that whatever you ask the Father in my name he may give you. This I command you: love one another.'*"

Jn 15:1-17

What is a friend?

The Bible, in the Book of Ecclesiastes, contains the following description of a friend.

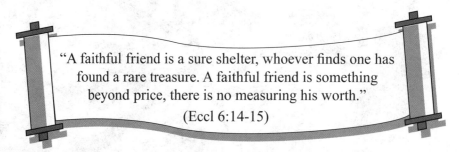

"A faithful friend is a sure shelter, whoever finds one has found a rare treasure. A faithful friend is something beyond price, there is no measuring his worth."

(Eccl 6:14-15)

What do you think of this description?

Think of your best friend and then write your own description of what a good friend is for you:

_____
_____
_____
_____

Draw a blue circle around the things a good friend does, and a red circle around the things a bad friend does:

- Keeps any secrets I tell him
- Makes fun of me in front of others
- Listens to me when I am feeling down
- Tells lies to hurt me
- Stands up for me when others speak badly of me
- Happily shares his things with me
- Forgives me when we've had some misunderstanding

- Plays with me only when I give him something in exchange
- Is happy with me when I enjoy some achievement
- Gets mad when things go better for me than for him
- Criticizes me and tells my secrets to others when I'm not around

Jesus wants to be your friend

- He has revealed to you all his teachings in the Gospel.
- He trusts you.
- He wants you to help him save all people.
- He invites you to his kingdom so that you can be happy with him forever.
- He gave his life for you so you can be saved.

How can you respond to this friendship?

_____
_____
_____
_____

Ways to build a friendship

Suppose you were to see someone at school you didn't know but with whom you'd like to be friends. Which of the following do you think would be good ways to start a friendship with that person? Draw a circle around them.

- Ask him his name
- Go up and push him
- Join in the game he is playing
- Ask him if he wants to play with you
- Act like a fool to get his attention

What can I do to build my friendship with Jesus?

Write down what these children are doing to be Jesus' friend.

_____   _____   _____

Jesus says that I'm his friend when I keep the commandments

What Jesus wants more than anything else is to make his Father happy. His Father is happy when we are happy. We are happy when we choose the road he marked out for us in the Ten Commandments.

Do you remember the Ten Commandments? Fill in the missing words.

1. You shall love the Lord your _____ above all _____.
2. You shall not _____ the name of the _____ your God in vain.
3. You shall keep _____ the Sabbath.
4. You shall honor your _____ and your _____.
5. You shall not _____.
6. You shall not commit impure _____.
7. You shall not _____.
8. You shall not _____ or give false _____.
9. You shall not consent to _____ thoughts or _____.
10. You shall not _____ your neighbor's goods.

Jesus summed up these Ten Commandments in:

•You shall love the Lord your God above all things. This commandment sums up the first three commandments, which speak of how we are to show our love for God.
•You shall love your neighbor as yourself. This commandment sums up Commandments four through ten, which speak of how we are to love our neighbor.

Jesus gave us a New Commandment, the commandment of love.
Write it down here:

_____

_____

The one who could have been Jesus' friend but said he couldn't.

Look up in the Gospel of Matthew the story of the rich young man (Mt 19:16-22) and find out what Jesus told him he needed to do to gain eternal life. Draw a picture here of the rich young man with Jesus.

I can't go to heaven if I am not Jesus' friend.

Jesus was very serious when he said, "Without me you can do nothing." He knows how weak we are and how many temptations the devil puts in our way to make us fall. Jesus knows that we need the strength that comes from being his friend if we want to be victorious to the end. That's why he tells us

"Whoever remains in me, and I in him, will bear much fruit."

Draw a line connecting the phrases on the left with correct matching phrases on the right.

If I am Jesus' friend

If I am not Jesus' friend

- I will make others happy.

- I will go to heaven.

- I will be selfish.

- I'll be able to overcome temptations.

- It'll be hard for me to do good.

- I'll bear much fruit.

- The devil will trick me easily.

- I will win many souls for God.

- I'll be in danger of going to hell forever.

- I will love others.

Write down how you can show Jesus you're his friend by the way you treat

your parents:_____

_____

your siblings: _____

_____

your friends:_____

_____

others: _____

_____

Don't forget

• Jesus wants you to be his friend.

• Jesus knows that separated from him you can't bear any fruit.

• Jesus points out the way to being his friend: "Love others as I love you."

• Jesus has told you that the greatest friend is the one who gives up his life for his friends.

Knowing my faith

List the Ten Commandments

1. You shall love the Lord your God above all things.
2. You shall not take the name of the Lord your God in vain.
3. You shall keep holy the Sabbath.
4. You shall honor your father and your mother.
5. You shall not kill.
6. You shall not commit impure acts.
7. You shall not steal.
8. You shall not lie or give false witness.
9. You shall not consent to impure thoughts or desires.
10. You shall not covet your neighbor's goods.

How did Jesus sum up the Ten Commandments?

He summed them up in two: You shall love the Lord your God above all things, and your neighbor as yourself.

Living my faith

• I'm going to keep in mind that my friendship with Jesus is the most important thing in my life. And I'm going to show him I realize this by loving others since that's what makes him happiest.

• I'm going to pray an Our Father every night, asking God to help me love others and to save me from falling into the devil's traps.

The Last Supper
Chapter 6
Review

Match up the two columns.

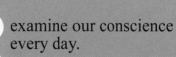

1. Man's only true happiness is found

2. Jesus teaches us that the greatest person

3. To see if we're on the right road, we should

4. These are signs Jesus left us to help us:

5. Jesus left us a New Commandment:

6. Jesus entrusted the Sacraments to

7. The greatest gift Jesus left us was the

8. The miracle by which bread and wine become the Body and Blood of Jesus:

9. Jesus teaches us that to bear fruit we must

10. To be Jesus' friends we have to

11. The greatest of friends is the one who

◯ examine our conscience every day.

◯ the sacraments.

◯ the Church.

◯ Eucharist.

◯ is the one who serves others.

◯ Transubstantiation.

◯ keep the commandments.

◯ gives up his life for others.

◯ remain united to him.

◯ in God.

◯ the Commandment of Love.

Study the following words:

Patient; Helpful; Ecclesial; Transubstantiation; Remain; Fruits

Now fill in the missing letters:

__ a __ ie __ t; H __ l __ f __ l; E ___ __ l __ s ___ __ l; Tr __ ns __ bst __ nt ___ __ t __ o __;

R __ ma __ n; __ r ___ t __ .

The Passion

Chapter 7

Father, if it is possible

Jesus' Prayer
Chapter 7, Lesson 1

Remember
the only way you can show God you really love him is by doing his will.

Now you're going to
Jesus obeyed his Father in order to save us.

The Gospel tells us

"Then Jesus came with them to a place called Gethsemane, and he said to his disciples, *'Sit here while I go over there and pray.'* He took along Peter and the two sons of Zebedee, and began to feel sorrow and distress. Then he said to them, *'My soul is sorrowful even to death. Remain here and keep watch with me.'* He advanced a little and fell prostrate in prayer, saying, *'My Father, if it is possible, let this cup pass from me; yet, not as I will, but as you will.'* When he returned to his disciples he found them asleep. He said to Peter, *'So you could not keep watch with me for one hour? Watch and pray that you may not undergo the test. The spirit is willing, but the flesh is weak.'* Withdrawing a second time, he prayed again, *'My Father, if it is not possible that this cup pass without my drinking it, your will be done!'* Then he returned once more and found them asleep, for they could not keep their eyes open. He left them and withdrew again and prayed a third time, saying the same thing again. Then he returned to his disciples and said to them, *'Are you still sleeping and taking your rest? Behold, the hour is at hand when the Son of Man is to be handed over to sinners. Get up, let us go. Look, my betrayer is at hand.'*"

Mt 26:36-46

What emotions does Jesus experience in this passage?

- **Sadness and grief:** he feels the sins of the world come over him.
- **Anguish:** he knows he is going to suffer and be killed.
- **Loneliness:** his friends are unaware of what is happening to him and so are unable to support him.

The Gospel tells us that Jesus asked the same thing of His Father three times.

Write down what he asked him._____

_____

What else did Jesus say to his Father?_____

_____

What do these words of Jesus mean?_____

_____

Can you recall a time when you experienced one of these emotions?

_____

_____

The Passion of Our Lord began in the Garden of Gethsemane. His physical passion, the sufferings of his body, would come later, ending with his death on the cross. In the Garden he endured the passion of his heart, interior suffering in which he responded before his Father, for all mankind's sins, taking them on himself as if they were his own. He did this to redeem us and to open for us the way to salvation. Jesus suffered anguish as he beheld the sins of all men, every offense ever committed against the love of God. Jesus saw how terrible those sins were and how heavily they would press down on him.

Jesus took upon himself all our sins, all our acts of selfishness and envy, hatred and anger, laziness and pride, every sin each one of us has ever committed, in order to save us and open heaven to each one of us.

Jesus begged his Father, if it were at all possible, to free him from drinking that bitter chalice. In spite of this, however, he conquered all his emotions and feelings, and embraced his Father's will.

What does Jesus tell us in the Gospels about the Will of God?

Look up the following verses and explain them in your own words:

John 4:34
_____

Matthew 6:10
_____

Matthew 7:21
_____

Matthew 12:50
_____
_____

We all experience many emotions and feelings in life, feelings such as joy and sadness. These emotions are good if they move us, guided by our reason and will, to do good.

By his prayer in the garden, Jesus teaches us to do God's will regardless of what we may feel anguish, sadness, loneliness, or pain.

In this situation:	what would a young person do to fulfill God's Will?	to ignore God's will?
When he is very tired and still has his homework to do.		
When a friend he doesn't really like wants to play with him.		
When his brother wants to play with his favorite toy.		
When he is watching TV and his mother asks him to help her with something.		
When he is very mad because he thinks something is unfair.		
When it's almost time to go to Communion and he's very hungry and wants to eat a piece of candy.		
When he has to tell the truth and stand up for something.		
When he hasn't studied and has the chance to cheat on a test.		

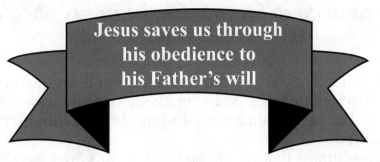

Jesus saves us through his obedience to his Father's will

In Romans 5:19 we read:

> **"As by one man's disobedience (Adam's) many were made sinners, so by one man's obedience (Jesus') many will be made righteous."**

According to this verse, why was Jesus' obedience important?

_____

_____

In your life, too, obedience is the path to doing God's will.

By obeying the Father and offering yourself up to him as Jesus did in the Garden of Gethsemane, you can collaborate with him in saving mankind.

Write some intentions for which you can offer up your acts of obedience:

1. _____

_____

2. _____

_____

3. _____

_____

Here are some other intentions for which you can offer up your acts:

• peace in the world
• the unity of all Christians
• the conversion of sinners
• vocations to the priesthood

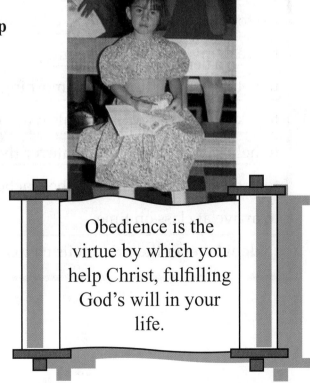

Obedience is the virtue by which you help Christ, fulfilling God's will in your life.

What do I need to do to imitate Christ in his obedience to the Father?

Study the following list. They are resolutions children like yourself have made because they want to imitate Jesus by being obedient as he was. As you will see, they are not unusual or super-human resolutions. Simple though they are, they have great merit before God.

Pick out the five resolutions that would be hardest for you. Check them off and resolve to carry them out this week out of love for God. You'll see they aren't so hard after all, and you'll be more like Jesus!

	This week I resolve
to obey my mother without delay.	
to do my homework at the time I should.	
to turn off the TV when it's time to study.	
to get up when my alarm goes off in the morning.	
to brush my teeth after meals.	
to go right to bed when it's bedtime.	
to stop playing when I'm asked to do something.	
to wash my hands before eating.	
to get dressed in time in the morning.	
to take all my school materials with me to school.	
to help my parents with whatever they ask of me.	
to keep quiet in class when the teacher tells us to.	
to arrive at class on time.	
to do whatever the priest tells us to at Mass.	

My Father!

How many times did Jesus say these words in the Garden of Gethsemane?_____

Jesus placed his needs and petitions before his Father. What were they?_____

_____

_____

_____

In the Garden, Jesus prayed with filial love, as a suffering son praying to the Father who could help him. Yet the will of his Father was what Jesus always obeyed as the most important thing.

You, too, like Jesus, can pray in this filial manner to God, your Father, presenting him all your needs and the needs of others. Whenever you do so, God will listen to your petitions and answer you in one way or another, either by taking care of the problem or giving you the strength to carry on. Just as in following his commandments God always gives us the graces we need to follow his will.

Don't forget always to say, like Jesus, **"May *your* will be done!"**

Don't forget about the example Mary gave us. She was always united to God through prayer and was always ready to do his will.

In the space provided write a prayer to God, presenting him your needs and the needs of others. End your prayer with Jesus' words: "May your will be done!"

_____

_____

_____

_____

_____

Don't forget

- Jesus saved us through his obedience.
- The most important thing for Jesus was to fulfill his Father's will.
- We need to obey God regardless of our feelings.
- We should pray full of filial confidence, trusting in God our Father, who loves us.
- By obeying God we collaborate with Jesus in the salvation of mankind.

Knowing my faith

What is the example of perfect prayer that we are given in the New Testament?
Jesus' prayer to his Father.
What does Jesus teach us about prayer?
He teaches us to pray to our Father in heaven with faith, trust, humility, and constancy.
What does Jesus teach us to seek in prayer?
He teaches us to seek the will of God.

Living my faith

- Jesus left me an example of obedience throughout his life. I'm going to think about when I find it hard to obey and make a special effort to obey at those times, offering it up to God for _____.
- I'm going to go to the chapel to pray to Jesus. Contemplating him on the cross, I'm going to ask him to help me obey even when I find it very hard.

And the Cock Crowed Three Times

Peter's Denial
Chapter 7, Lesson 2

Remember
**God is always ready
to forgive us.**
Now you're going to see
**God's mercy
is greater than any sin.**

The Gospel tells us

"Now Peter was sitting outside in the courtyard. One of the maids came over to him and said, *'You too were with Jesus the Galilean.'* But he denied it in front of everyone, saying, *'I do not know what you are talking about!'* As he went out to the gate, another girl saw him and said to those who were there, *'This man was with Jesus the Nazorean.'* Again he denied it with an oath, *'I do not know the man!'* A little later the bystanders came over and said to Peter, *'Surely you too are one of them; even your speech gives you away.'* At that he began to curse and to swear, *'I do not know the man.'* And immediately a cock crowed. Then Peter remembered the word that Jesus had spoken: *'Before the cock crows you will deny me three times.'* He went out and began to weep bitterly."

Mt 26:69-75

Using the Gospel as a guide, write what is happening in each drawing on the line provided.

Who is Peter?

Look up the following Gospel passages and connect them to their meaning.

John 1:42

Luke 5:10

Matthew 16:18-19

Luke 22:31-32

John 21:15-19

• Jesus tells Peter that he will be in charge of the Church.

• Jesus prays for Peter so that his faith will not fail.

• Jesus calls Peter to be a fisher of men.

• Jesus gives him the name "Peter" and singles him out.

• Jesus questions Peter on his love.

**What do these passages tell us?
Fill in the blanks:**

_____ was Jesus' very _____ friend. Jesus _____ him many things and entrusted his _____ to him.

Peter • Church • taught • special

Do you have a very special friend?

How would you feel if:
• you told him a secret and he turned around and told the whole world?
• you asked him to help you and he refused?
• you found out he was speaking badly of you?
• he told others he wasn't your friend, that he didn't care about you at all?
• you did everything you could for him and he ignored you?

Write down how you would feel

_____

_____

_____

_____

Do you remember how Judas Iscariot betrayed Jesus' friendship? You already know what happened afterwards. Write it down here.

_____

_____

_____

_____

Peter also "betrayed" Jesus when he denied him three times.

Remember the very special love Jesus had for Peter. Which betrayal do you think was worse, Peter's or Judas'? _____
Why?_____

Was there any difference between Peter's betrayal and Judas'?

Judas
Jesus chose him to be his friend.
Judas betrayed this friendship.

Peter
Jesus chose him to be his friend.
Peter betrayed this friendship.

One thing's for sure. Their lives ended very differently. Draw lines to show how different the reactions and results were between Peter and Judas.

Judas

- Gave in to despair.
- Did not trust in the mercy of Jesus.
- Trusted in the love and mercy of his best friend.
- Love for his master led him to true conversion.
- He hanged himself.
- Became a great saint.

Peter

Where did Peter place his trust?

In chapter 15 of St. Luke's Gospel, Jesus speaks to us of the mercy of God which is always ready to forgive sinners. Jesus tells us three parables.

A sheep gets lost and its shepherd goes off in search of it. He is overjoyed when he finds it because he loves each one of his sheep very much.
In heaven there is more joy over one sinner who repents than over ninety-nine just men who have no need of repentance.

Parable of the lost sheep, Lk 15:3-7

Parable of the lost coin, Lk 15:8-10

A woman loses a coin. She searches her whole house and when she finds it she goes and tells all her friends because she is so happy about having found it.
Thus there will be joy among the angels of heaven over one sinner who repents.

A father's youngest son had left home, and the father finally sees him returning. The father runs to meet him and embrace him. He throws a feast because his son has come back home.
We should celebrate and rejoice because this brother was dead and has come back to life; he was lost and is found.

Parable of the prodigal son, Lk 15:11-32

Never forget that God wants us all to go to heaven. That's why Jesus came to earth. God's mercy is greater than any sin.

The Gospel tells us that Peter wept.
Why do you think he wept?_____

_____

To repent we first have to know what sins we've committed. (Recall the examination of conscience, Chapter Six, Lesson 1.) Once we are aware of the sins we've committed we need to repent from our hearts, just as Peter did.

Perfect contrition: This is the remorse we feel for having sinned because we are grieved over having offended God who is our Father.

Imperfect contrition: This is sorrow over our sins caused by fear of eternal punishment in hell.

What did Peter do after he wept over his sin?

He was faithful to his prayer-life.

He received the Holy Spirit at Pentecost.

He was head of the Twelve Apostles from the beginning.

He performed miracles in Jesus' name.

He spoke before the Sanhedrin.

He baptized Gentiles.

He died as a witness to his faith. Today St. Peter's Basilica, the center of Catholicism, stands over the place he died.

We are a lot like Peter

1. We are Jesus' very special friends.
2. We are chosen by Christ.
3. We are called to be saints.
4. There may be times when we betray Jesus by sinning.
5. We trust in Christ's mercy.
6. We repent and resolve to change.
7. We seek Jesus' forgiveness in confession.

After seeking out Jesus, Peter repented and amended his life. Recall that the third step to a good confession is a firm purpose of amendment. Write what this means in your own words:

_____

_____

To amend, or change yourself for the better, you need to fight constantly against sin. Better yet, you need to strive constantly towards holiness, taking concrete steps to overcome whatever takes you away from God.

Recall the seven capital sins. Every sin we commit has its source in one of the capital sins. Write them down here:_____

_____

Think of a temptation someone your age might face and write it down:

_____

_____

Now think about how Jesus would confront this temptation. Write it down here:

_____

_____

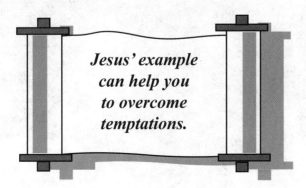

Jesus' example can help you to overcome temptations.

Don't forget

- God's mercy will always be greater than your sins.
- You should always have full trust in your friend, Jesus, and never give in to discouragement or despair.
- God is moved by the remorse and sorrow we feel for having offended him.
- Always maintain an attitude of total trust in God's forgiveness, take the necessary steps to improve every day, and thank God for his mercy.

Knowing my faith

What is perfect contrition?
It is the remorse we feel for having sinned because we are grieved over having offended God who is our Father.

What is imperfect contrition?
Sorrow over our sins caused by fear of eternal punishment in hell.

What is "firm purpose of amendment"?
It is the determination to overcome sin and to take concrete steps for doing so.

Living my faith

- I'm going to go to Jesus in the sacrament of Confession, asking him to forgive me and help me change as Peter did.
- I'm going to get a friend to go to confession and trust in God's mercy.
- I'm going to carefully draw up a plan of action to overcome my faults and be a better person. I'm going to review my plan every day to see how I'm doing.

Mary and John

Mary at the Foot of the Cross
Chapter 7, Lesson 3

Remember
Mary was always faithful to God's will for her.
Now you're going to see
Jesus gave us Mary to be our Mother, and that in her we have a great example to follow.

The Gospel tells us
"Standing by the cross of Jesus were his mother and his mother's sister, Mary the wife of Clopas, and Mary of Magdala. When Jesus saw his mother and the disciple there whom he loved, he said to his mother, *'Woman, behold, your son.'* Then he said to the disciple, *'Behold, your mother.'* And from that hour the disciple took her into his home."

Jn 19:25-27

> **Break into small groups with your classmates. Discuss the following ideas together and then tell the whole class what your group thinks.**
>
> - Despite the difficulties, Mary was faithful to God from the moment of the Annunciation to Christ's death on Calvary.
> - Mary is co-redeemer with Christ, collaborating with him in our Redemption.
> - Jesus wanted to share Mary with us so that we would turn to her as our Mother, just as he did.
> - Mary is the Mother of Christianity. John represents all people of all times whom Christ came to save.

What does Mary do for us?

Mary is our Mother. She is there to help and assist us in everything. She is always watching out for our needs, just as our earthly mother does.

Moreover, Mary is our Mother in the order of grace. All the graces and gifts God sends us come through her hands. She presents to God all our intentions and prayers.

We need to trust in Mary. Are you familiar with what the Virgin of Guadalupe said to Juan Diego when he was worried about how things would go?

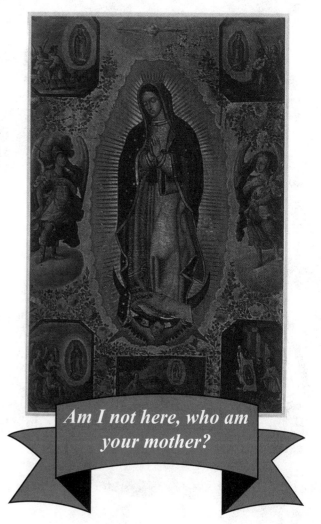

Am I not here, who am your mother?

And all nations will call me blessed

We honor Mary and acknowledge her as our loving Mother and protector. We do this in many ways. Here are some of them.

1. Celebrating Marian Feastdays

Do some research and find out the dates of the following feastdays and then match up the two columns:

◯ January 1st	1. The month dedicated to the Holy Rosary
◯ March 25th	2. The Feast of the Assumption
◯ August 15th	3. The Birth of Mary
◯ September 8th	4. The month dedicated to Mary
◯ December 8th	5. The Feast of the Immaculate Heart of Mary
◯ The Saturday following the Feast of the Sacred Heart of Jesus	6. The Feast of Mary, Mother of God
◯ May	7. The Feast of the Immaculate Conception
◯ October	8. The day of the week dedicated to Mary
◯ Saturday	9. The Feast of the Annunciation

Devotion to Mary has inspired many great artists to create masterpieces in her honor.

2. Marian shrines - the Blessed Virgin around the world

Research the following Marian shrines and indicate where they are in the world using the numbers.

1. Lourdes   2. Fatima   3. Carmen   4. Czestochowa   5. Guadalupe
6. Pilar   7. Loretto   8. Lujan   9. Coromoto
10. National Shrine of the Immaculate Conception

Write down any others you know about and put them on the map.

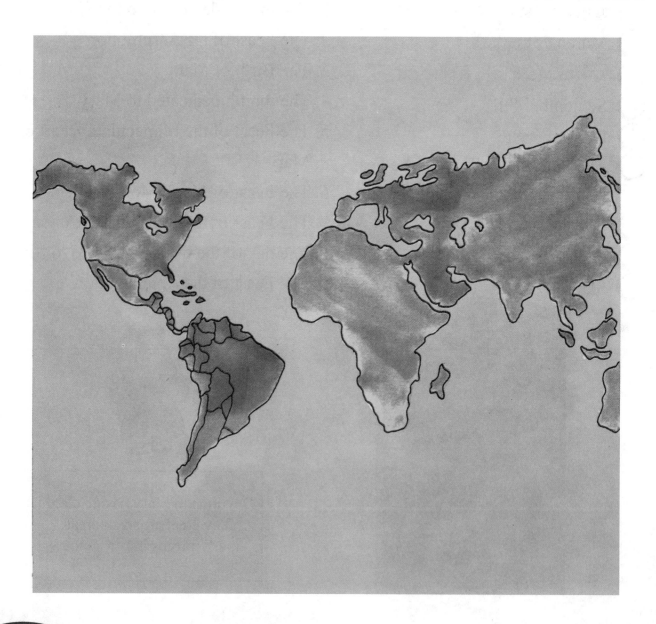

"And John took her into his home"

We too, should welcome Mary into our homes and venerate her.

Think for a moment and ask yourself the following questions.

- Is there a picture or statue of Mary in your house?
- Do you remember her often?
- Do you greet her when you come and go?
- Do you pray to Mary every day?
- Do you feel true love and devotion for her?
- Do you place all your needs in her maternal hands?
- Does Mary has a special place in your life?

True devotion to Mary consists in imitating her virtues.

Look up the following Gospel passages and write down the virtues Mary shows in them.

Luke 1:26-38
What virtues do you see in Mary?

_____

_____

Luke 1:39-56
What virtues do you see in Mary?

_____

_____

Luke 2:15-20
What virtues do you see in Mary?

_____

_____

John 2:1-11
What virtues do you see in Mary?

_____

_____

On March 25, 1984, before Our Lady of Fatima, Pope John Paul II consecrated the world to the Immaculate Heart of Mary.

How alike are you and Mary?

The way to show our love for Mary is by imitating her virtues.

Write a brief paragraph explaining how you can imitate Mary in one of her virtues.

_____

_____

_____

_____

_____

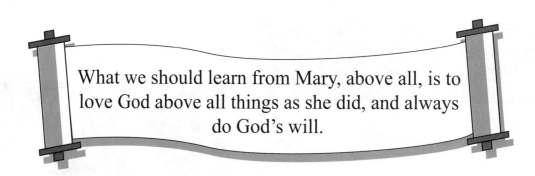

What we should learn from Mary, above all, is to love God above all things as she did, and always do God's will.

Practicing devotion to Mary
The Holy Rosary

St. Dominic, to whom Mary appeared, is said to have been the first one to spread the practice of praying the rosary.

Mary herself is chief among those to spread the practice of praying the rosary. At Fatima, she asked the three children to pray it every day.

The Church has always encouraged us to pray the rosary. Mary, in her apparitions all over the world, asks us to pray the rosary every day.

The rosary is a way to honor Mary and tell her how much we love her, while at the same time recalling the mysteries of Jesus' and Mary's lives.

The Joyful Mysteries
Prayed on Mondays and Saturdays

1._____
2._____
3._____
4._____
5._____

The Sorrowful Mysteries
Prayed on Tuesdays and Fridays

1._____
2._____
3._____
4._____
5._____

The Glorious Mysteries
Prayed on Wednesdays and Sundays

1._____
2._____
3._____
4._____
5._____

The Luminous Mysteries
Prayed on Thursdays

1._____
2._____
3._____
4._____
5._____

Don't forget to pray the rosary every day. It is Mary's path to lead us to heaven. If you don't already pray the rosary you can start with one decade a day. Another way is to pray five decades each day, but saying three Hail Marys for each decade, and gradually increasing until you pray the full ten Hail Marys.

Don't forget

- In a wholly singular way Mary cooperated by her obedience, faith, hope, and burning charity in Christ's work of salvation.
- From the cross, Jesus gave us Mary to be our Mother.
- Mary is Mother of the Church. She longs to help us in everything, especially in living the life of grace and getting to heaven.
- True devotion to Mary consists in imitating her virtues, especially her openness to God's will and her faithfulness in carrying it out.

Knowing my faith

How does Mary help us as our heavenly Mother?
By being a living example for us and by obtaining from God the graces we need.

In what does true devotion to Mary consist?
Imitating her virtues.

What prayers do we have for honoring Mary?
The Hail Mary and the Holy Rosary are the most well-known.

What is the rosary?
It is a form of prayer that honors Mary; during it we meditate on the chief mysteries of the life of Jesus and Mary.

Living my faith

- I'm going to think of ways I can imitate Mary's virtues at home, at school, and with my friends.
- I'm going to resolve to do something each day that will help me to be more like Mary.
- I'm going to pray a decade of the Rosary every day, offering it up for the needs of my family and the whole world, especially so that more and more people will go to heaven accompanied by Mary.
- I'm going to make a visit to Mary with one of my friends.

And We Keep Doing the Same

"Father, Forgive them"
Chapter 7, Lesson 4

Remember
Jesus came to earth to save us.

Now you're going to see
**we are all very important to God,
and he wants us all to be saved.**

The Gospel tells us

"When they came to the place called the Skull, they crucified him and the criminals there, one on his right, the other on his left. Then Jesus said, *'Father, forgive them, they know not what they do.'* They divided his garments by casting lots. The people stood by and watched; the rulers, meanwhile, sneered at him and said, *'He saved others, let him save himself if he is the chosen one, the Messiah of God.'* Even the soldiers jeered at him. As they approached to offer him wine they called out, *'If you are King of the Jews, save yourself.'* Above him there was an inscription that read, *'This is the King of the Jews.'* Now one of the criminals hanging there reviled Jesus, saying, *'Are you not the Messiah? Save yourself and us.'* The other, however, rebuking him, said in reply, *'Have you no fear of God, for you are subject to the same condemnation? And indeed, we have been condemned justly, for the sentence we received corresponds to our crimes, but this man has done nothing criminal.'* Then he said, *'Jesus, remember me when you come into your kingdom.'* He replied to him, *'Amen, I say to you, today you will be with me in Paradise.'*"

Lk 23:33-43

Spend some time looking at a crucifix or a picture of Jesus' crucifixion. Then answer the following questions; afterwards, discuss your answers with your classmates.

How do you think Jesus felt as people stood by and made fun of him?

_____

How did he feel being crucified together with thieves?

_____

Why did Jesus, although he was innocent, accept dying on the cross?

_____

What do these words mean: "Father, forgive them because they know not what they do"?

> *Jesus died for all men. We are all important to him.*

We are all very different people. We all have a mission. God loves us all.

Make up a small biography for each of these persons.

Claudia, fourth-grade student:
_____
_____
_____

Ann, housewife and mother of four:
_____
_____
_____

Father Richard, priest:
_____
_____
_____

John, run-away:
_____
_____
_____

Tony, juvenile delinquent:
_____
_____
_____

Jane, fourth-grade teacher:
_____
_____
_____

We are all sinners, God loves each of us, and Jesus died to save us.
We aren't "something" God created, but rather "someone" very important to him.

Look up Mark 10:45. What was Jesus' mission? Write it down here and discuss it with your classmates.
_____
_____

Jesus shed his blood for one and all, so that we could all go to heaven. Remember, that is our goal. That's why we were created, to be happy with God forever.

Look up Matthew 18:14. Copy it in the space below, and discuss its importance with your classmates.

God wants us all to get to heaven. With the help of his grace and the merits Jesus won for us on the cross, we can get there if we do our part.

The formula is very simple:

Repentant sinner + the love and grace of God + merit won by Jesus

= salvation and holiness.

They know not what they do

On the cross, Jesus bore our sins, forgave us and interceded for us before God. He knew and knows that we don't realize how serious it is when we:

- sin because of our lack love, as if we made Christ's cross heavier.
- offend others through our lack of charity
- don't worry about overcoming sin, thinking that everything is all right.
- fail to help others out of laziness or indifference.

In the space below, write some other attitudes you can think of for which Christ asks us to be forgiven.

_____
_____
_____
_____
_____
_____

Jesus took upon himself all the sins of mankind, the sins of all people and all times. Can you imagine what that would be like?

From now on whenever you face a temptation, remember that your sins, no matter how small, come to weigh on Christ as he hangs on the cross.

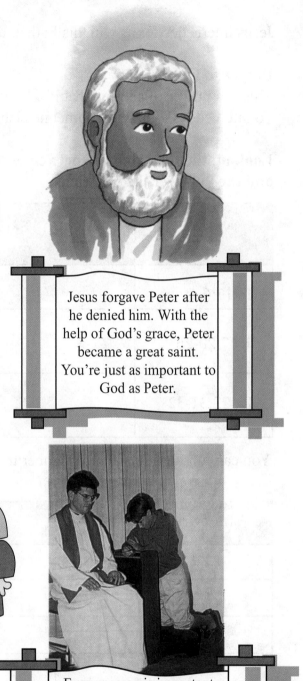

Jesus forgave Peter after he denied him. With the help of God's grace, Peter became a great saint. You're just as important to God as Peter.

Every person is important to God. He wants all of us to get to heaven--that's what he created us for. Through the sacrament of Confession we regain the state of grace, essential for getting to heaven.

Jesus intercedes for us with his Father, and he teaches us to pray for others, too.

Prayer of intercession
This is a prayer of petition that is a lot like Jesus' prayer, the Our Father.
To intercede is to pray for someone else, for the needs of others.

**Look up the following Gospel verses. Read them carefully
and then answer the questions.**

Verses	For whom is Jesus praying?	What does he ask the Father to do?
Jn 17:6-19		
Jn 17:20-26		
Lk 22:31-32		

You can imitate Jesus and remember the needs of others every day in your prayers.

Who can you pray for?	What can you ask God to do for them?

Remember also that by offering up your daily
activities, and carrying them out the best you can
out of love for God, you help make reparation
for the sins of the world.

One who followed Jesus' example

Stephen was a man of great faith. The apostles had chosen him to be one of the very first deacons. The deacons of that time went around taking care of the elderly, orphans, and the Christian community in general. This left the apostles free to pray and preach the Word of God.

Stephen was full of power and grace, working wonders among the people. Some non-believers took Stephen to task for his belief in Christ, but they could not match his wisdom and power. So they brought Stephen before the Sanhedrin where false witnesses accused him of speaking against the Law.

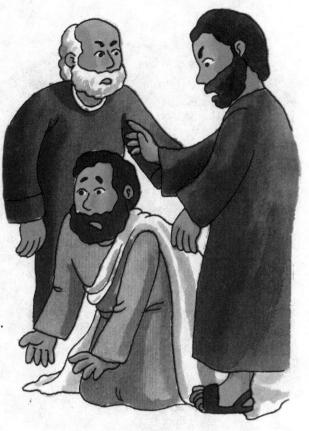

Stephen responded by reminding them of the history of the people of Israel, beginning with God's appearance to Abraham. Israel, Stephen pointed out, had killed all the prophets God had sent to reveal his will. Then Stephen suddenly saw Jesus in the clouds above him, at the right hand of God the Father, and he told his accusers what he saw. When they heard it they sprang on him and dragged him out to stone him.

A young man named Saul was there. He approved of the stoning and looked after the coats of those who did the stoning. This young man later became St. Paul.

Just before dying, Stephen prayed for those who killed him, just as Jesus did from the cross.

"Father," Stephen cried out, *"do not lay this sin against them."*

St. Stephen was the first martyr in the history of Christianity. He was the first one to die for his faith. He taught us how we can imitate Christ by forgiving others and praying to God for them.

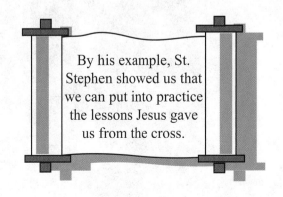

By his example, St. Stephen showed us that we can put into practice the lessons Jesus gave us from the cross.

Don't forget

• Jesus died to save all men. We are all important to him.
• He died out of love for us, because he wants us to get to heaven.
• While on the cross, Jesus taught us to forgive others.
• Jesus interceded for us before God and he teaches us to pray for others through the prayer of intercession.

Knowing my faith

Why did Jesus die on the cross?
The Scriptures teach us that Jesus died on the cross because of our sins.

Why did Jesus accept dying on the cross?
To show his love for his Father and for all men, redeeming us from sin.

What did Christ's death achieve?
It opened to us the way to forgiveness and salvation.

Living my faith

• I am very important to God, so much so that Christ shed his blood to save me. I'm going to care for this dignity of being God's child by doing my best this week to live as he wants me to live.
• I'm going to forgive anyone who wrongs me, just as Jesus taught me.
• I'm going to visit Jesus in the chapel and pray for the needs of all people, before praying for myself.

The Passion of Christ
Chapter 7
Review

Match the two columns.

1. Christ's Passion began...

2. In prayer we should seek the fulfillment of...

3. Our model of perfect prayer should be...

4. God's mercy is always greater than...

5. Remorse over having offended God is...

6. Remorse over fear of punishment is...

7. A great way to imitate Mary is to...

8. Jesus left us his Mother...

9. The Church honors Mary by...

10. Praying for others is...

11. Jesus died on cross to save...

12. The first martyr ever was...

◯ to intercede for them.

◯ imperfect contrition.

◯ Jesus' prayer to his Father.

◯ our sins.

◯ all men.

◯ in the Garden of Gethsemane.

◯ imitate her virtues.

◯ from the cross.

◯ God's will.

◯ perfect contrition.

◯ St. Stephen.

◯ praying the Holy Rosary.

Study the following words:

Intercession; Contrition; Despair; Repentance; Co-redeemer.

__ nt __ rc __ ss __ __ n; C __ n __ r __ t __ o __ ; D __ sp __ __ r; R __ p __ n __ a __ c __ ;

C __ -r __ d __ __ __ m __ r.

The Resurrection

Chapter 8

Why do you seek him among the dead?

The Resurrection
Chapter 8, Lesson 1

Remember
Jesus triumphed over death and sin.

Now you're going to see
Christianity is a religion of joy.

The Gospel tells us

"After the Sabbath, as the first day of the week was dawning, Mary Magdalene and the other Mary came to see the tomb. And behold, there was a great earthquake; for an angel of the Lord descended from heaven, approached, rolled back the stone, and sat upon it. His appearance was like lightning and his clothing was white as snow. The guards were shaking with fear of him and became like dead men... Then the angel said to the women *'Why do you seek the living one among the dead? He is not here, but he has been raised. Remember what he said to you while he was still in Galilee, that the Son of Man must be handed over to sinners and be crucified, and rise on the third day?'* And they remembered his words. Then they went away quickly from the tomb, fearful yet overjoyed... And behold, Jesus met them on their way and greeted them. They approached, embraced his feet, and did him homage. Then Jesus said to them, *'Do not be afraid. Go tell my brothers to go to Galilee, and there they will see me.'* They then ran to announce this to his disciples..."

Mt 28:1-10; Lk 24:5-8

Activity

Notice the different attitudes adopted by the people in this account of Jesus' Resurrection:

- **The Angel**   Serene, for he knew that what Jesus had said would come true.
- **The Soldiers**   Were overcome with fright and fainted.
- **The women**   Became overjoyed and ran to tell the disciples.

Draw in the boxes the people named, showing how they reacted to Jesus' Resurrection:

Soldiers	*The Angel*	*The Women*

Now draw yourself next to the Risen Jesus, showing your reaction to his Resurrection: indifferent, fearful, happy or serene?

If Jesus hadn't risen from the dead

- *His life would have been a failure.*
- *His words would have lost their credibility.*
- *His promises would have gone unfulfilled.*
- *We wouldn't know if he was really God.*
- *Our lives, as disciples of an impostor, would be meaningless.*

But Jesus did rise from the dead

- *He overcame death and sin!*
- *Jesus is God!*
- *We, too, will one day rise from the dead!*
- *He won eternal life for us!*
- *Our whole lives have meaning!*

This is why

we, too, are victorious, and we should show it!

How should we show it?

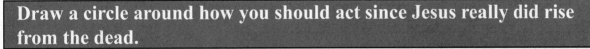

Draw a circle around how you should act since Jesus really did rise from the dead.

- Be afraid of death, thinking there is nothing beyond it.

- Be pessimistic, thinking that nothing, including my life, has any meaning.

- Do my homework happily, even when I don't feel like it, knowing this will help me get to heaven.

- Be joyful, knowing that God wants me to be happy forever with him in heaven.

- Be happy, even when I'm sick, knowing that suffering will help me get to heaven.

Easter: The most important feast of all

There are many very important feastdays in the Church. Indicate what the following feastdays celebrate by connecting the columns:

- Holy Thursday   • Jesus' entry into Jerusalem
- Christmas   • The institution of the Eucharist
- Pentecost   • Our Lord's Resurrection
- Epiphany   • Jesus' birth
- Easter   • The descent of the Holy Spirit upon the apostles
- Palm Sunday   • Jesus revealed as the Savior of all men

All these feastdays are important, but the most important of them all is Easter, the celebration of Our Lord's Resurrection.

Easter is the "Pascal Feast," the feast of the Passover, in which we celebrate Jesus' passing from death to life.

Easter begins on Holy Saturday night with the Easter Vigil Mass, which is made up of the following parts:

• The blessing of the fire and of the Easter candle
The fire symbolizes the victory of light over darkness, of life over death. The Easter candle symbolizes Christ risen from the dead. We hold lighted candles as a sign that we are called to enlighten others with our faith and good works.

• The Easter Proclamation
We proclaim Christ's Resurrection, by which death is conquered by life.

• Liturgy of the Word
A series of readings recounting Salvation history. The joy of the Resurrection is expressed by singing the Gloria and the Alleluia.

• The Baptismal Rite
Water is blessed and baptisms are celebrated. All those present renew their baptismal promises and recite the creed.

• Liturgy of the Eucharist
We participate in the Eucharist in commemoration of Jesus' death and resurrection.

The Easter season lasts for 50 days; it begins with the Easter Vigil Mass and ends with the Feast of Pentecost.

How do we celebrate Easter at home, as a family?

One of the first things you probably think of when you think of Easter is "Easter eggs." They are the ones we color and paint, as well as chocolate and candy eggs we give and receive as gifts. This is a very ancient custom and it came about in the following way.

In ancient Egypt the Egyptians used to give each other decorated eggs on special occasions. They decorated them with colors they extracted from plants, and the more ornate the egg, the better the gift it represented. After receiving them as gifts, the Egyptians would display them in their homes as decorations.

After Christ rose from the dead and ascended to heaven, the first Christians developed the idea of fixing a time of preparation before Easter. It came to be called Lent. It lasted forty days, during which time everyone would make sacrifices and purify themselves so as to celebrate Easter more worthily. One of the sacrifices they made was not to eat eggs during the 40 days.

Lent ended on Easter Sunday. Since they hadn't eaten eggs all through Lent, when Easter Sunday arrived people would walk the streets with baskets of eggs to give away as gifts as a sign of their joy over Christ's Resurrection.

Then one day someone remembered what the Egyptians used to do and decided to paint the eggs he was going to give away. The idea caught on and other people starting doing the same. So from that time on, people have given gifts of colored eggs on Easter Sunday as a reminder that Christ rose from the dead, and we, too, will one day rise to eternal life. In time other kinds of eggs appeared, such as the chocolate and candy eggs we have today.

God wants us to live forever and has given us a sacrament by which we pass from the death of sin to risen life in Christ, becoming children of God with heaven as our inheritance.

Do you remember the name of this sacrament?

Fill in the missing letters:

B __ __ __ __ __ M

Don't forget

- Christianity is a religion of joy because Jesus rose from the dead, overcoming death and sin.
- Jesus lives forever and awaits us in heaven.
- Jesus rose from the dead. We know that we, too, will rise from the dead.
- Jesus' Resurrection is what gives meaning to our lives.
- Easter is the most important feast of the Church.
- At Easter, the Passover Feast, Jesus passes from death to life.
- Through baptism, we Christians pass from the death of sin to risen life in Christ.

Knowing my faith

What is the Church's most important feast?
Easter is the most important feast.
What do we celebrate at Easter?
We celebrate Our Lord's Resurrection.
What day is Easter celebrated?
The Sunday after Good Friday.
Why is Jesus' Resurrection so important?
Because it gives meaning to everything in our lives, our work, suffering, and even death.
What are the historical proofs for Jesus' Resurrection from the dead?
The empty tomb and Jesus' appearances to the disciples over a period of forty days.
Who were the first witnesses of Jesus' Resurrection?
The holy women who went to anoint Jesus' body.

Living my faith

- I'm going to make the most of the ceremony my catechism teacher is going to organize to renew our baptismal promises. During it I'm going to keep in mind that God wants me to live forever and that keeping my baptismal promises is essential to reaching eternal life.
- Even though it's not Easter, I'm going to color some eggs and give them away as gifts to my friends and my family, telling them the history and meaning of Easter eggs.

They didn't recognize him!

The Disciples of Emmaus
Chapter 8, Lesson 2

Remember the Mass has different parts, each with its own special meaning.

Now you're going to see there is a passage in the Gospels that follows the same order as the Mass!

The Gospel tells us

"Now that very day two of them were going to a village seven miles from Jerusalem called Emmaus, and they were conversing about all the things that had occurred. And it happened that while they were conversing and debating, Jesus himself drew near and walked with them, but their eyes were prevented from recognizing him. He asked them, *'What are you discussing as you walk along?'* They stopped, looking downcast. One of them, named Cleopas, said to him in reply, *'Are you the only visitor to Jerusalem who does not know of the things that have taken place there in these days?'* And he replied to them, *'What sort of things?'* They said to him, *'The things that happened to Jesus the Nazarene, who was a prophet mighty in deed and word before God and all the people, how our chief priests and rulers both handed him over to a sentence of death and crucified him. But we were hoping that he would be the one to redeem Israel; and besides all this, it is now the third day since this took place. Some women from our group, however, have astounded us: they were at the tomb early in the morning and did not find his body; they came back and reported that they had indeed seen a vision of angels who announced that he was alive. Then some of those with us went to the tomb and found things just as the women had described, but him they did not see.'* And he said to them, *'Oh, how foolish you are! How slow of heart to believe all that the prophets spoke! Was it not necessary that the Messiah should suffer these things and enter into his glory?'* Then beginning with Moses and all the prophets, he interpreted to them what referred to him in all the scriptures. As they approached the village to which they were going, he gave the impression that he was going on farther. But they urged him, *'Stay with us, for it is nearly evening and the day is almost over.'* So he went in to stay with them. And it happened that, while he was with them at table, he took bread, said the blessing, broke it, and gave it to them. With that their eyes were opened and they recognized him, but he vanished from their sight. Then they said to each other, *'Were not our hearts burning within us while he spoke to us on the way and opened the scriptures to us?'* So they set out at once and returned to Jerusalem where they found gathered together the eleven and those with them who were saying, *'The Lord has truly been raised and has appeared to Simon!'* Then the two recounted what had taken place on the way and how he was made known to them in the breaking of the bread."

Lk 24:13-35

Fill in the blanks using the words provided.

The two disciples were _____.   *running*

Jesus began to _____ with them.   *late*

They didn't _____ him.   *breaking of bread*

Jesus explained the _____ to them.   *sad*

Since it was already _____ they invited him to dinner.   *vanished*

They recognized him in the _____.   *recognize*

Jesus _____ from their sight.   *walk*

The disciples went _____ to tell the others.   *Scriptures*

Do you remember the different parts of the Mass?

Fill in the missing letters. If you need help, see Chapter 2, Lesson 1.

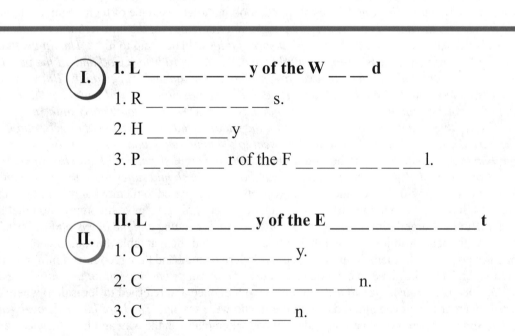

I.   **I. L** _ _ _ _ _ **y of the W** _ _ **d**

1. R _ _ _ _ _ _ s.

2. H _ _ _ _ y

3. P _ _ _ _ r of the F _ _ _ _ _ _ _ l.

II.   **II. L** _ _ _ _ _ _ **y of the E** _ _ _ _ _ _ _ _ **t**

1. O _ _ _ _ _ _ y.

2. C _ _ _ _ _ _ _ _ _ _ _ n.

3. C _ _ _ _ _ _ _ n.

Remember

During the Liturgy of the Word, the Word of God is read and explained.
During the Liturgy of the Eucharist, bread and wine are offered up to God and then consecrated, becoming the Body and Blood of Christ. After that, Holy Communion is distributed to the faithful.

Do you see a similarity between the parts of the Mass and the Gospel passage about the disciples of Emmaus? Respond below.

_____

_____

Think back on how the disciples of Emmaus reacted to Jesus when he accompanied them. Read the following statements and write either TRUE or FALSE after each one:

They ignored Christ when he came up to them. _____

They listened carefully to all that Christ had to say. _____

They invited him to eat with them. _____

They told him to go on his way. _____

They recognized him in the breaking of bread because they were paying attention. _____

They were distracted and so didn't see anything special when the bread was broken. _____

Look at the following drawings and draw a star underneath the picture of the children who are behaving like the disciples of Emmaus.

After Holy Communion comes the final blessing in which the faithful are
sent to fulfill the will of God in their daily lives.
This "fulfilling of God's will" is the "mission" of the faithful, and from there comes
the word, "Mass."

"Go in peace to love and serve the Lord."

Circle the correct answers.

What did the disciples do after Jesus vanished from their sight?

• They went into shock.
• They fell asleep.
• They kept eating as if nothing had happened.
• They started talking about other things.
•They got right up and went to tell the others.

What do you do when you leave church after Mass?

• I tell my mom to buy me some candy.
• I start giving my brothers and sisters a hard time.
• I don't do anything, I just sit there quietly.
• I leave ready to be a witness of Christ.

How they were rewarded

Because they had the right attitude, the disciples of Emmaus received many rewards:

• Their sadness was gone.

• They clearly understood what had happened to Jesus.

• They enjoyed Jesus' divine company.

• They felt their hearts "burning" with joy.

• They recognized Jesus in the breaking of bread.

• They were given the strength to go and announce Jesus' Resurrection to the others.

If you want to enjoy these same rewards

• Put an end to sadness in your life and place your hopes and dreams in Christ.

• Make a real effort to understand Jesus' teachings.

• Always preserve Jesus' presence in your soul.

• Live with contagious joy.

• Speak often with Jesus in the Eucharist.

• Be dedicated in carrying out your mission as a witness of Christ.

You can do all of this at Mass, living every moment of it close to Jesus.

Don't forget

- The disciples of Emmaus received many rewards because they knew how to make the most of the brief time they had with Jesus.
- You can obtain these same rewards if you make the most of every Mass you attend.

Knowing my faith

Why is the Eucharistic celebration called the "Mass"?
Because at the end of the Mass the priest sends out the faithful to carry their "mission" as witnesses of Christ.

What kind of dispositions should you cultivate during Mass?

1. Attentiveness during the readings and the homily
2. Devotion and adoration during the Consecration
3. Readiness to fulfill the will of God during the Offertory and Communion

What fruits are obtained from participating in the Mass correctly?
Five main fruits are obtained: an understanding of the Word of God; increased faith for recognizing Jesus; joy and interior peace; Jesus' presence in my soul; and, the strength to carry out my mission.

Living my faith

- I'm going to attend Mass this Sunday with the dispositions necessary for obtaining all the fruits it offers me.
- I'm going to encourage everyone in my family to live the Mass with great love for God, just as he wants us to do.

Go and Teach All People

The Apostles' Mission
Chapter 8, Lesson 3

Remember
**God needs your hands,
your feet, your lips.**

Now you're going to see.
**Jesus gave his
apostles a special mission.**

The Gospel tells us
"The eleven disciples went to Galilee, to the mountain to which Jesus had ordered them. When they saw him, they fell down to worship him, though some hesitated. Then Jesus approached and said to them, *'All power in heaven and on earth has been given to me. Go, therefore, and make disciples of all nations, baptizing them in the name of the Father, and of the Son, and of the Holy Spirit, teaching them to observe all that I have commanded you. And behold, I am with you always, until the end of the age.'"*

Mt 28:16-20

Activity

Jesus took one of his final moments with his disciples to give them a very important message.

Use the following code to decipher it:

A	B	C	D	E	F	G	H	I	J	K	L	M
Α	Β	Χ	Δ	Ε	Φ	Γ	Η	Ι	ϑ	Κ	Λ	Μ

N	O	P	Q	R	S	T	U	V	W	X	Y	Z
Ν	Ο	Π	Θ	Ρ	Σ	Τ	Υ	ς	Ω	Ξ	Ψ	Ζ

"ΓΟ ΤΗΕΡΕΦΟΡΕ ΑΝΔ ΜΑΚΕ ΔΙΣΧΙΠΛΕΣ ΟΦ ΑΛΛ ΝΑΤΙΟΝΣ ΒΑΠΤΙΖΙΝΓ ΤΗΕΜ ΙΝ ΤΗΕ ΝΑΜΕ ΟΦ ΤΗΕ ΦΑΤΗΕΡ ΑΝΔ ΟΦ ΤΗΕ ΣΟΝ ΑΝΔ ΟΦ ΤΗΕ ΗΟΛΨ ΣΠΙΡΙΤ ΤΕΑΧΗΙΝΓ ΤΗΕΜ ΤΟ ΟΒΣΕΡςΕ ΑΛΛ ΤΗΑΤ Ι ΗΑςΕ ΧΟΜΜΑΝΔΕΔ ΨΟΥ."

" _____ , _____ , _____
_____ , _____
_____
_____ , _____
_____ ____ _____ "

Read the following statement. Cross out with a red line the ones that are not part of what Jesus commanded his disciples to do.

• Jesus wanted his disciples to keep his teachings a secret.

• Jesus wanted his disciples to be a leaven to transform the dough of the world.

• Jesus sent his disciples out to do apostolate.

• Jesus told them to preach only to the Jews.

• He sent them to preach the Gospel to the whole world.

• He asked them to stay home so that no one would see them.

• He instructed them to baptize all men in the name of the Holy Trinity.

Remember

You too are called to do apostolate, to spread the Gospel seed in hearts everywhere, and to be leaven in the world, transforming it through your example.

Through baptism you have come to share in three of Christ's very important functions. Find them in this alphabet soup:

(If you can't remember them, go back to Lesson 3 of Chapter III.)

```
A S D E F R G R A U K I
P R A E R D O T E X Z U
P R I E S T E F G Y R D
A T Y E G F F G B N K H
F R J K I N G T S F H U
S A Z R R F V B N H U I
D E P R O P H E T L O P
```

Using the words you just found, fill in the blanks below with the correct answers.

I fulfill my _____ functions by making all my actions sacred.

I fulfill my _____ functions by preaching the Gospel with my words and actions.

I fulfill my _____ functions by learning to govern, or master, myself, and by changing the things I can so that they are in agreement with God's will.

You are an indispensable link in the chain of salvation

Can you imagine what would have happened if the apostles hadn't carried out their mission of preaching the Gospel to all men?

Jesus' mission would have been thwarted, for he came to save all men. If the apostles hadn't gone out preaching, very few would have been able to be saved. Jesus needed the apostles to carry on his mission of saving all men.

And now Christ, in the very same way, ***needs you!*** He needs you to lend him your hands, your feet, your lips, your tongue, your heart, so that all men may come to know him and reach heaven.

You have a very important mission to carry out where God has placed you: in your family, among your friends, in your daily activities. There are many souls that need you in order to get to know Christ, and no one can take your place in carrying out the specific mission God has given you.

Finish this chain of salvation by drawing yourself and writing your name, followed by the souls that are close to you and in need of your help to get to heaven.

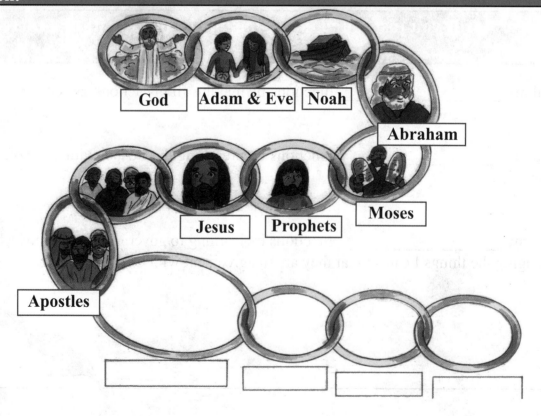

God | Adam & Eve | Noah

Abraham

Jesus | Prophets | Moses

Apostles

Why don't you do something for Jesus?

The story of a boy who complained to God.

A priest once told the story of a boy who one day went to the chapel to speak with Jesus. Sad and upset, he said to Jesus:

"I don't understand you, Jesus. I know you're good and all-powerful, and that you love us all very much because you even died for us. But when I look around me and see everything that's happening in the world, I get the feeling you just don't care. There's war, hatred, injustice, broken families, children dying of hunger, and kids hooked on drugs.
"If you love us so much, Jesus, why don't you make people know you and love you so that all the evil in the world will come to an end? Why don't you do something, Jesus?!"

Then the boy heard a voice:

> *"I **have** done something. I created you."*

You could have been that boy. Jesus has chosen you, too, to preach his Word to all people and to help bring to an end all the evil in the world. Jesus is counting on you!

Draw a picture of some problem in the world you can help to solve through your words, actions, and example.

Don't forget

Christ needs you so that his mission to save all men will not be frustrated.

Knowing my faith

Learn the following prayer and say it every morning.

Lord Jesus,
I give you my hands to do your work.
I give you my feet to follow your path.
I give you my eyes to see as you see.
I give you my tongue to speak your words.
I give you my mind that you may think in me.
I give you my spirit that you may pray in me.
Above all I give you my heart that in me you may love your Father and all people.
I give you my whole self that you may grow in me;
so that it is you, Christ, who live and work and pray in me.
Amen.

Living my faith

This week I'm going to see the people close to me as souls God has placed in my life so that I can help them attain salvation. These are the things I'm going to do to keep this commitment:

_____
_____
_____
_____

And he went up into the clouds...

The Ascension
Chapter 8, Lesson 4

Remember
Jesus rose from the dead,
overcoming death and sin, so we
could enjoy heaven forever.

Now you're going to see
Jesus ascended to heaven and is
waiting for us there.

The Gospel tells us

"Then he led them out as far as Bethany, raised his hands, and blessed them. As he blessed them he departed from them and was taken up to heaven. They did him homage and then returned to Jerusalem with great joy, and they were continually in the temple praising God."

Lk 24:50-53

Fill in the blanks with the words on the right.

1. _____ ascended to _____ to be with his _____.
2. Jesus returns to heaven in _____ after having fulfilled his _____.
3. His mission was to win _____ _____ for us through his _____ and _____.
4. Jesus awaits us in heaven to live _____ _____ with him.

happy forever
heaven
Jesus
glory
mission
eternal life
Resurrection
Father
death

When he ascended to heaven, Jesus went home to be with his Father again. Can you imagine how he must have felt? How do you feel when you get home again after a long and tiring trip? Write it down here.

By rising from the dead Jesus conquered sin, and God's promise of salvation came true. From that moment on heaven, which is *our* home too, was opened to all of us.

My home on earth.

Location:_____
_____
Description:_____
_____
People who live there:_____
_____
My favorite thing about my house:_____
_____

My home in heaven.
Write a paragraph describing what you think heaven will be like:

_____
_____
_____
_____
_____
_____
_____
_____
_____

Heaven is the greatest gift we can receive. Jesus won it for us. Don't forget that heaven isn't a place, it's a state of being: total happiness with God.

Be sure, as part of your daily prayer, to take a few moments to thank and praise Jesus for this great gift.

We can turn every act of our lives into an expression of our gratitude to God.

We should praise God in prayer, not only because of what he has done for us, but also just because of who he is.

Write some things here that you can thank and praise God for every day:

1. _____
   _____
2. _____
   _____
3. _____
   _____
4. _____
   _____
5. _____
   _____

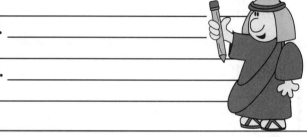

And never forget to thank God for the great gift of heaven, living in the joy and hope of the Risen Lord who will always help you on your way to heaven.

St. Thomas Aquinas

St. Teresa of Avila

St. Paul

God has allowed some saints to see heaven, and they've all said the same thing about it: **"Words could never express how wonderful it is!"**

Don't forget

- After completing his mission, Jesus ascended to heaven in glory to be with his Father forever as God and as man.
- Our true destiny is to live in heaven forever with Jesus.
- Our life now is a preparation for the life Christ won for us by his death and Resurrection.
- We need to thank Jesus for opening heaven to us, and we need to praise him because he is worthy of praise.

Knowing my faith

Who will we live with in heaven?
We will live forever with Christ.
What does Christ do for us from heaven?
He intercedes for us constantly with the Father.
What is prayer of thanksgiving?
It thanks God for everything he gave us, joy, suffering, success, failure.
What is a prayer of praise?
It is the prayer in which we praise and glorify God because he is God and because of what he has done.

Living my faith

- I'm going to take some time today to thank Jesus for all the following things: for having saved me, for waiting for me in heaven, for all the gifts he has given me, and for allowing me to get to know him better this school year.
- I'm going to pray to him for the grace to grow closer and closer to him, to love him more and live according to his Gospel.

The Resurrection of Christ
Chapter 8
Review

Match the columns.

1. Christianity is a religion of

2. Our lives have meaning because

3. The Church's most important feast is

4. The disciples of Emmaus recognized Jesus

5. The Eucharistic celebration is also called

6. One of the fruits of Mass is

7. Jesus promised to be with us

8. I am an indispensable link in

9. Jesus has given me the mission of

10. Jesus returned to being with his Father at the

11. Jesus won heaven for us by his

12. Praying and glorifying God

○ prayer of praise.

○ in the breaking of bread.

○ Ascension.

○ Jesus rose from the dead.

○ Easter

○ joy in one's heart.

○ until the end of the world.

○ death and Resurrection.

○ the chain of salvation.

○ Mass.

○ joy.

○ being his witness before all men and leading them to him.

Study the following words:

Resurrection; Disciples; Ascension; Mission; Salvation.

Now fill in the missing letters:

R __ s __ rr __ ct __ __ __ n; D __ sc __ pl __ s; A __ __ __ e __ __ __ io __ __; __ i __ __ __ io __ __; S __ lv __ t __ __ __ n.